Databases

with Access

Learning Made Simple

Moira Stephen

Routledge
Taylor & Francis Group

LONDON AND NEW YORK

First published 2006 by Elsevier Ltd.

First published 2017 by Routledge
2 Park Square, Milton Park, Abingdon, Oxon OX14 4RN
711 Third Avenue, New York, NY 10017, USA

*Routledge is an imprint of the Taylor & Francis Group,
an informa business*

First issued in hardback 2017

British Library Cataloguing in Publication Data
A catalogue record for this book is available from the British Library

ISBN-13: 978-0-7506-8186-5 (pbk)
ISBN-13: 978-1-138-43632-9 (hbk)

Typeset by P.K.McBride, Southampton

Icons designed by Sarah Ward © 1994

Contents

Preface

The books in the Learning Made Simple series aim to do exactly what it says on the cover – make learning simple.

A Learning Made Simple book:

◆ Is **fully illustrated**: with clearly labelled screenshots.

◆ Is **easy to read**: with brief explanations, and clear instructions.

◆ Is **task-based**: each short section concentrates on one job at a time.

◆ **Builds knowledge**: ideas and techniques are presented in the right order so that your understanding builds progressively as you work through the book.

◆ Is **flexible**: as each section is self-contained, if you know it, you can skip it.

The books in the Learning Made Simple books series are designed with learning in mind, and so do not directly follow the structure of any specific syllabus – but they do cover the content. This book covers Module 5 of the ECDL syllabus and the Database aspects of New CLAIT. For details of how the sections map against your syllabus, please go to the website:

http://www.madesimple.co.uk

1 Getting started

What is a database?

A database is simply a collection of data, stored in an organised way. For example, it may be:

◆ an address list

◆ employee details

◆ details about items in stock.

A simple database could be used to store the names and addresses of those you send Christmas cards to, or details of your CD collection. A more complex database could be used to store the data that you need to run your company, e.g. supplier, customer, stock and order details.

Database jargon

If you have never used a database before, you might not have encountered some of the database terminology that we will use in this book. Here are brief definitions of the terms you will come across.

Table: All the data on one topic is stored in a table. A table could contain details of the employees that work for your company. In a simple database, you might have only one table. More complex ones may consist of several tables.

Record: The data for a single item in a table is held in that item's record. Using the employee table example, each employee would have their own record within the employee table.

Field: A field is a piece of information within a record e.g. in your employee table, things like surname, job title, date of birth, or salary grade.

Field name: The label, or name, given to a field.

Primary key: A special field that will contain a unique piece of information in each record e.g. StaffID.

Relationship: A relationship is used to link two tables through a common field.

Tip

If you have never used a database package before, I suggest you read through the next few pages carefully. Database concepts and jargon are not difficult, but you need to appreciate how a database works and to become familiar with some of the jargon you will come across. If you're already familiar with databases, move on to 'Getting into Access' (page 12).

Join: The process of linking two tables is often referred to as joining them.

Data definition: The process of defining, or describing, the data to be stored. This will involve specifying the data type (text, number, date), the field size, and how it is related to other tables.

Data manipulation: This term describes any work done on existing data within your tables. Sorting and extracting data and producing reports from it would all be examples of data manipulation.

Company database file

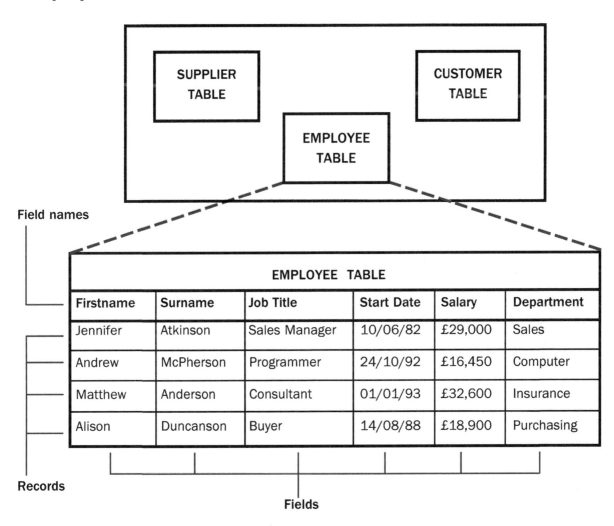

Access objects

There are seven different types of objects in Access - Tables, Queries, Forms, Reports, Pages, Macros and Modules.

We will use four of these objects – Tables, Queries, Forms and Reports – as we progress through this book.

Tables

Tables are used to store your data. You can enter and edit your data in the table datasheet – which looks very similar to an Excel worksheet.

Main purpose: Store, input and edit data

Queries

Queries are used to extract data from your tables. You might want to extract data using a specific criterion, e.g. all staff that work in a specific department.

Main purpose: Extract data

Forms

Forms are used for data entry and editing. They provide a 'user friendly' interface with your tables.

Main purpose: Input and edit data

Reports

Reports are used to display your data in a meaningful way, ready for printing.

Main purpose: Extract data, lay data out ready for printing

So there are two objects that you can use to enter and edit your data – tables and forms. The data is actually stored in the table.

And there are two objects that you can use to extract data from your tables – queries and reports.

Tip

Learn to recognise these tabs – they can speed up your work.

Preparing your data

The most important (and often difficult) stage in setting up your database takes place away from the computer. Before you set up a database you must work out how your data should be organised. Ask yourself two key questions:

◆   What do I want to store?

◆   What information do I want to get out of my database?

NB: You must also work out your answers to these!!

Once you've decided what you are storing and what use you intend to make of the data, you are ready to start designing your database. Again, much of this can be done away from the computer.

What fields do you need?

You must break the data down into the smallest units you want to search or sort on. Each of these must be in a separate field.

If you were setting up **names**, you would probably break the name into three fields – Title, Firstname (or Initials) and Surname. This way you can sort the file into Surname order, or search for someone using the Firstname and Surname.

If you were storing **addresses**, you would probably want separate fields for Town/city, Region and/or Country. You can then sort your records into order on any of these fields, or locate records by specifying appropriate search criteria. For example, using Town/city and Country fields, you could search for addresses in Perth (Town/city), Australia (Country) rather than Perth (Town/city), Scotland (Country).

The number of lines in an address can vary considerably, e.g. 12 High Street, Edinburgh, EH22 (with one address line before the town) vs. The Old Schoolhouse, East Lane, Cranshaws, Nr Duns, Borders Region, TD10 (where you have three address lines before the town).

Tip

When planning your database, take a small sample of the data to be stored and examine it carefully. Break the detail on each item into small units for sorting and searching. You can then start to work out what fields will be needed to enable you to store all the necessary data for each item.

When creating your tables set up enough fields to accommodate a full address (perhaps by using an Address 1, Address 2, and Address 3 field) before you get to the town, postcode etc. When entering data into address fields the Address 1 field should always be used, the Address 2 and Address 3 could be used if necessary. Make sure you always enter the town, postcode, county etc. into the same field in each record.

How big are the fields?

You must also decide how much space is required for each field. The space you allocate must be long enough to accommodate the longest item that might go there. How long is the longest surname you want to store? If in doubt, take a sample of some typical names (McDonald, Peterson, MacKenzie, Harvey-Jones?) and add a few more characters to the longest one to be sure. An error in field size isn't as serious as an error in record structure as field sizes can be expanded without existing data being affected.

It is very important that you spend time organising and structuring your data before you start to computerise it – it'll save you a lot of time and frustration in the long run!

You can edit the structure of your table if necessary – but hunting through existing data to update records is time consuming, so it's best to get it right to start with!

Take note

You can specify the size of text and number fields.

Text fields can be up to 255 characters in length (the default is 50). Numbers which are just used as identifiers, e.g. codes or telephone numbers, should be stored in text fields.

Number fields should be used for any numbers that you may want to perform calculations on. There are several size options for number fields (see Field Size in the on-line Help).

Normalisation

When deciding on the tables required, you should consider how best to group the fields to minimise the duplication of data throughout the database – this is what is meant by the process of *normalisation*.

For example, you may be setting up a database to record details of items that you keep in stock and the suppliers that you use.

You could record all this information in one table, with fields for stock code, item description, cost, supplier name, supplier address, supplier telephone number, contact name, etc. However, using one table may result in a lot of data duplication – if you get 200 stock items from the same supplier, you would need to add the supplier details into the record for each stock item – that means that the supplier information would have to be entered 200 times!!

The solution to this kind of problem is to *normalise* the data. As a result of normalisation, you end up organising your data fields into a group of tables, that can be combined when and as required.

In the stock example, you could create two tables. One could hold details of the stock item, e.g. code, description, colour, supplier code, etc. The other could hold all the supplier information – supplier code, company name, contact name, address, telephone number, etc.

The information on each supplier would be entered just once – into the supplier table. In the stock table, the supplier would be identified using the supplier code. The two tables could be linked through the supplier code, so that the data from both tables can be combined. So if you do have the same supplier for 200 stock items, you only need to enter the supplier details once!

There are several benefits to this approach:

◆ Each set of details (supplier) is stored (and therefore keyed in) only once.

◆ The stock table will be considerably smaller in size than it otherwise would have been.

◆ Should any of the supplier details change (phone number/ address) you only have one record to update (in the Supplier table).

◆ If you wrongly identify a supplier in a record in the Stock table, you have only one field to correct in each record that contains the error, rather than several fields.

Take note

On page 10 we introduce a project (based around a bookshop) that you can set up to help you learn how to use Access and practise the features that are introduced in this book. In the project the tables required and table structures have been worked out for you.

The project has been kept simple, as it would be impractical in a book of this size to discuss every table, form and report you might need. Although desirable in a real database, a stock control system to show how many copies are in stock and their values, a form for pre-ordering, etc. have not been included.

Most records will have an identifier - a field that holds a unique piece of information in each record in the table.

In a Staff table, each member of staff would have a different StaffID, so the primary key would usually be the StaffID (or Staff Number). The field that contains the staff name, or department may hold the same information in several records - there might be three employees called John Smith, or 20 employees working in the Sales department. But each one of them would have their own, unique, StaffID.

In a table that stored details of company cars, the car registration field would be the primary key - each car would have a different registration number. Your company might have several BMWs as company cars, but each one would have its own, unique, registration number.

Once a field has been set as the primary key you cannot enter duplicate information into it - Access will not allow it.

Database design

Before you start to create a database on your computer, you should take some time to design it. You need to work out what fields you will need, and how you will group them into tables. You will also want to identify the primary key in each table, and decide how your tables will be related to each other.

We will use an example of a database that might be set up for your local book store.

Take note

At beginner/intermediate level you might not be asked to design a database yourself – you will be given the design to work with. However, an appreciation of how the design was reached can be useful, so do take time to read through this section. If you are an intermediate/advanced user you will nearly always need to be able to design your own database.

Take note

In Chapter 2, you will be given a database design to set up for practice.

Book shop example

Let's say that you wanted to create a database to store details of the books in your book shop. You decide that you want to store the following information on each book:

    ISBN (a unique number given to each book published)

    Book Title   Author name   Price

    Classification (fiction/non-fiction/science/travel etc)

    Year published Publisher name   Publisher address

    Publisher contact

To maximise the sorting and searching capabilities of your database, this list could be extended and broken down into the following fields:

ISBN	Book Title	
Author Firstname	Author Surname	
Price	Classification	Year published
Publisher name	Publisher contact person	
Publisher address 1	Publisher address 2	
Town	Region	Country
Postcode	Telephone no.	Email

You could put all of these fields in one table. However, this would lead to a potentially inefficient database as you would have to repeat the publisher details in each record for every book that you bought from that publisher (perhaps resulting in the same data being entered hundreds of times).

As we are really storing information on two different things here - the book, and the publisher - we should set up two tables - one for information on the book and one for information on the publisher. When working with databases, the things that you store information on (and usually end up having a table for) are sometimes called *entities*.

The fields identified so far belong to the tables as follows:

Tip

These first few pages have introduced you to some of the jargon and theory that are associated with databases.

At this stage, don't worry if you can't really understand everything that you have read – but come back to this section and read it again and again as you use Access.

It's often easier to appreciate the theory once you have seen it in action!

Book table

ISBN
Book Title
Author Firstname
Author Surname
Price
Classification
Year published

Publisher table

Name
Contact person
Address 1
Address 2
Town
Region
Country
Postcode
Telephone number
Email

In the Book table, we would want to be able to identify which company published the book – so we should add the Publisher name field to the Book table – or, better still, a PublisherID field. We should also add a PublisherID field to the Publisher table. This field would be the primary key field in the Publisher table – each publisher would have a unique ID. The ISBN would be the primary key field in the Book table – each book would have a unique ISBN. The tables would be linked through their common field – the PublisherID field.

So our final database design would be:

Book table

ISBN (primary key)
Book Title
Author Firstname
Author Surname
Price
Classification
Year published
PublisherID

Publisher table

PublisherID (primary key)
Name
Contact person
Address 1
Address 2
Town
Region
Country
Postcode
Telephone number
Email

We still have to finalise details of the data types and properties of each field, but the basic design has been established.

Getting into Access

It is assumed that Access is already installed on your computer. If it isn't, you must install it (or get someone else to install it for you) before going any further.

◆ If you are already working in another application, save any files that you want to keep, close the application(s) you are working in and return to the Desktop.

You're now ready to start using Access.

You can start Access through the Start Menu on the Taskbar or from the Microsoft Office Shortcut Bar (if you have it displayed).

Basic steps

■ **From the Taskbar**

1 Click the **Start** button on the Taskbar.

2 Point to **All Programs**.

3 Point to **Microsoft Office**.

4 Click on **Microsoft Office Access 2003**.

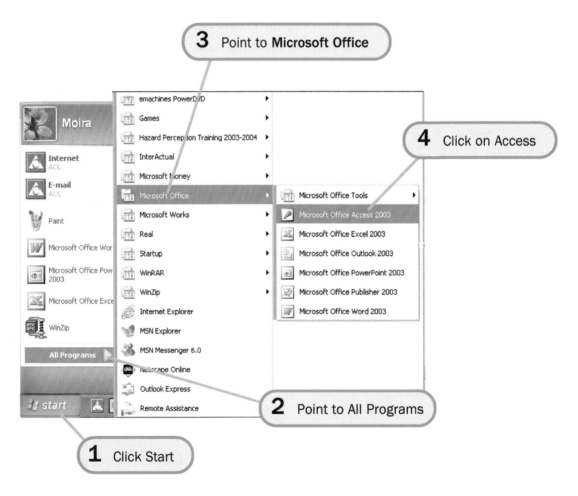

3 Point to **Microsoft Office**

4 Click on Access

2 Point to All Programs

1 Click Start

The Access screen

Take note

Access, like other Office applications, personalises your menu and toolbars. You can expand the menus to reveal all commands. After you select a command, or click a button on the toolbar, it appears on your personalised menu or toolbar. Toolbars can share space in a single row on the screen, so you have more room for your work.

Don't panic if your toolbars or menus are not exactly the same as those in the book!

Close the File New Database dialog box (click **Cancel**), so that you can view the Microsoft Access screen.

Looking at the Access screen, you can identify the standard elements of any Window: the Title bar, Menu bar and Toolbar; the Minimize, Maximize/Restore and Close buttons, and the Status bar.

I suggest you Maximize the Access window. This way other windows that may be open on your desktop won't distract you.

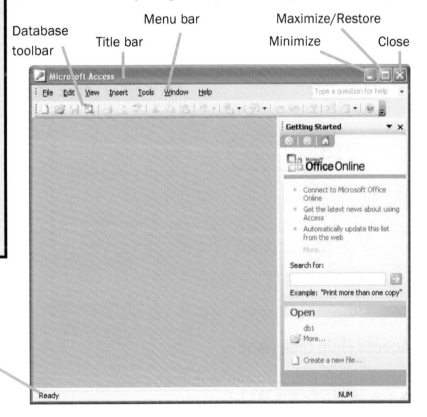

Exiting Access

When you have completed your session in Access, you must exit the package and return to the Windows environment (*don't* just switch off your PC!!). To exit, click the **Close** button ☒ on the Title bar or open the **File** menu and choose **Exit**.

13

Help

When working in Access, there is always plenty of Help available - the trick is being able to find it. There are several ways to get Help - most very intuitive and easy to use.

Type a question for Help box

You can reach the Help system using the Type a question box on the right of the menu bar.

Access Help task pane

The task pane is divided into three main areas:

- ◆ The Offline Help can be accessed from the **Search for:** field and the **Table of Contents** option in the top area.

- ◆ The Online Help can be accessed from the middle area.

- ◆ Specific areas such as 'What's New', 'Contact Us' and 'Accessibility Help' can be accessed from the **See also list** at the bottom of the task pane.

Basic steps

- ■ **Type a question**

1 Type in your question.

2 Press [**Enter**].

3 Choose a topic from the **Search Results** task pane – click on it.

- ■ **Display Help task pane**

4 Click the **Access Help** tool ⊙ on the Standard toolbar.

or

5 Press [**F1**].

14

Basic steps

- **Search**

1 Enter a keyword or keywords in the **Search for:** field at the top of the Access Help task pane.

2 Press **[Enter]** or to display a list of topics in the Search Results task pane.

3 Click on the topic that sounds most likely to display the Help page you want.

- **Browse**

4 Click the **Table of Contents** option near the top of the Help task pane.

5 Click on a book in the Table of Contents list – it will open to display other books or topics.

6 Open another book, or click on a topic to display its Help page.

Search for Help

You can also search another location in the Search options at the bottom of the Search Results task pane, or try searching for different keywords.

Table of Contents

You can browse through the Help available using the Table of Contents option.

You can adjust the width of the Table of Contents pane by dragging its left edge

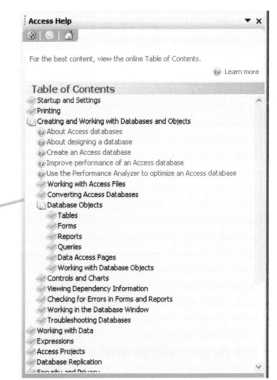

Take note

The Back , Forward and Home icons at the top of a task pane take you backwards and forwards through the panes that you have used recently, or Home to the Getting Started task pane that is displayed when you open Access.

Hot spots

On a Help page, some text may be blue. This indicates a 'hot spot' that can display some information. The most common types of hot spots are:

◆ Bulleted item - displays a list of instructions

◆ Embedded item - gives (usually in green) an explanation of the word or phrase

◆ Tip - suggested Help

◆ Show All - expands or collapses all the hot spots on the page.

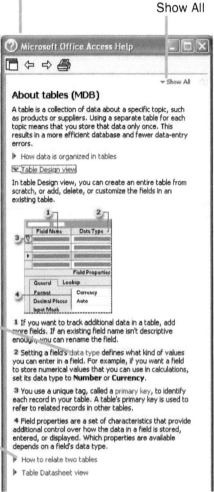

Show All

Embedded item

Bulleted item

Help page toolbar buttons

☐ Tiles the windows and the Help page panel.

☐ Undoes the tiling - and the button reverts to ☐ .

⇦ Takes you back through the Help pages viewed.

⇨ Takes you forward through the Help pages viewed.

🖨 Prints the Help page.

Basic steps

1 Open the **Help** menu.

2 Choose **Microsoft Office Online**.

3 Navigate your way through the Help pages until you find the information required.

If you cannot find the Help that you need in the normal Help system, visit the Microsoft Office Online site for updated Help files, answers to top support issues and frequently asked questions on Access, tips and templates.

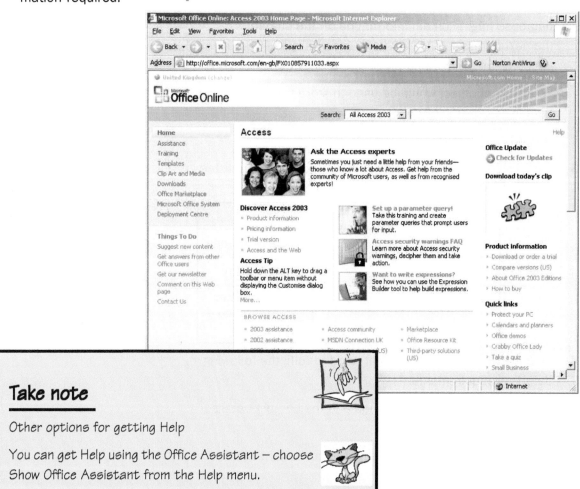

Take note

Other options for getting Help

You can get Help using the Office Assistant – choose Show Office Assistant from the Help menu.

In a dialog box, click the Help button 🛈, then click on the item within the dialog box that you want to find out about – a brief explanation of the item will be displayed

Exercises

1   Complete the following sentence, by filling in the gaps,
    using the words

    collection   **organised**   **stored**   **database**

    A _____ is a _____ of data, _____ on
    a computer in an _____, or structured, way.

2   A database can be used to store information on a number
    of related, albeit different, things. For example, a student
    database might contain information on the student
    (name/address, etc.) and the courses (title/level/certificat-
    ing body) that they could take.

    What sort of object would be used to store the student
    data in this example?

    Record   Field   Table

3   The objects that you will learn to use in this book are listed
    below. Match each object with its function.

Object			Purpose	
Report	1		A	Data Storage
Query	2		B	Data Entry
Table	3		C	Extract Data
Form	4		D	Print Data

4   Suggest which tables you might need to fulfil the following
    database requirements:

    The items of stock held in a shop and the contact details
    of the suppliers of that stock.

    A list of patients at a hospital and the consultant who is
    responsible for them.

    A list of the CDs held in a music store and details of the
    music company they were bought from.

5 To display the Microsoft Office Access Help panel you would click:

(a) ⊡ (b) ⊞ (c) 🐱 (d) ⊡

6 Display the **Help Table of Contents**, and open the **Startup and Settings** book. Go to the section on **Get Started with Access 2003**.

Read the information on **Using a database for the first time**, and **Databases: What they are and how they work**.

Alternatively, use the **Search** options to find out about what a database is and how it works.

7 Using the **Type a question for help** box, locate information on creating a database.

Read the section on **Create a database without using a Database wizard**.

List the steps involved in creating a new database using this method.

(a) ....

(b) ....

(c) ....

8 Use the Office Assistant to find out how to create a table in Design view. List the things that you can do to a table structure in this view.

(a) ....

(b) ....

(c) ....

9 Which function key displays the Access Help panel?

10 Locate Help on working in a table in datasheet view using the Access Help panel. Read the information that you find.

11 If you have Internet Access, go to Training on Microsoft Office Online and explore any topic that interests you.

Tip

If you can't find the Help that you need, click **Can't find it?** at the bottom of the Search Results Task Pane – Access will give you suggestions on how you could make your search more successful.

2 Building a database

Creating a database

When you first start Microsoft Access the Access window is displayed (see opposite), with the Getting Started task pane on the right-hand side. From here you can open an existing file or create a new one.

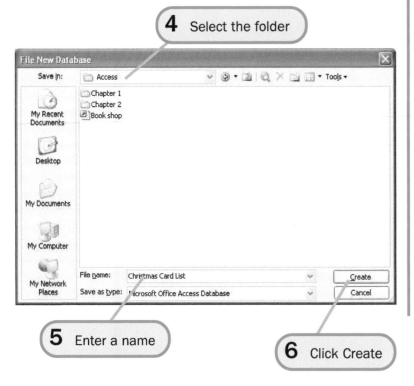

4 Select the folder

5 Enter a name

6 Click Create

1 Click [Create a new file...] on the **Getting Started** task pane.

or

2 Click the **New** tool [ ] on the Standard toolbar.

3 Click [Blank database...] on the **New File** task pane.

4 Select the folder that you wish to store your database in.

5 Give your database a name – 'Christmas Card List' in this example.

6 Click [Create].

7 Your database window will be displayed.

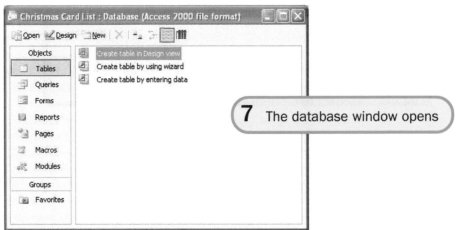

7 The database window opens

22

Basic steps

Opening a database

1 Start Access (if necessary).

2 Select the file from the **Open** list on the **Getting Started** task pane.

or

3 Open the **File** menu and choose the file from those at the bottom.

or

4 Click ☞ More... on the **Getting Started** task pane or the **Open** tool ☞ on the **Standard** toolbar.

5 Locate the folder that contains the database.

6 Select the database.

7 Click ☞ Open ▾ to open it.

Recently used files can be opened from the Getting Started task pane or the File menu. Older files must be opened through the Open dialog box.

Creating a table

Once you have created your database file, the next step is to create your table(s). A table consists of:

◆ The record structure – the field names, data types and properties, and

◆ The record data, e.g. publisher information

This database consists of ONE table only. The table will end up containing a list of names and addresses – your Christmas Card list.

The field names, data types and properties of each field are listed in the table below.

Field name	Data type	Properties
CCID	AutoNumber	Primary Key
Title	Text	Field Size = 10
First name	Text	Field Size = 20
Surname	Text	Field Size = 20
Address 1	Text	Field Size = 30
Address 2	Text	Field Size = 30
Town	Text	Field Size = 20
Region	Text	Field Size = 20
Postcode	Text	Field Size = 12
Tel No	Text	Field Size = 15
Email	Text	Field Size = 25

1 Select **Tables** in the Objects bar of the Database window.

2 Double-click  Create table in Design view .

Or

3 Click New in the Database window.

4 Select **Design View** in the **New Table** dialog box

5 Click **OK**.

Take note

We will be using Design view for the tables we create in this book.

4 Select Design View

5 Click OK

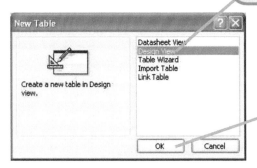

Data types

There are 10 different data types to choose from when setting up your table structures. The data types you will use most often are described here.

Data Type	Usage	Size	Notes
Text	Alphanumeric data	up to 255 bytes	Default data type
Number	Numeric data	1, 2, 4 or 8 bytes	
Date/Time	Dates and times	8 bytes	Date and time values for the years 100 through to 9999
Currency	Monetary data	8 bytes	Accurate to 4 decimal places and 15 digits to the left of the separator
AutoNumber	Unique long integer generated by Access for each new record	4 bytes	Cannot be updated; useful for Primary Key fields
Yes/No	Boolean data	1 bit	Fields that contain one of two values – Yes/No, On/Off, True/False.

Take note

Most of your fields will probably be Text, with a few of the others used in each table depending on the type of data you wish to store.

Properties

You can customise fields by specifying different properties. The properties most commonly used are listed here.

Take note

The properties depend upon the data type.

Property	Data Type	Notes
Field size	Text and Number	Text can have a field size from 1-255 (default is 50)
	Number field sizes are:	Values:
	Byte (single byte)	0 – 255
	Integer (2-byte)	–32,768 to 32,767
	Long Integer (4-byte)	–2,147,483,648 to 2,147,483,648
	Single (4-byte)	–3.4 x 1038 to 3.4 x 1038
	Double (8-byte)	–1.797 x 10308 to +1.797 x 10308
Format	Controls how data is displayed or printed	Options depend on data type
Decimal places	Number and currency	Auto (displays 2 decimal places for most formats) or fixed – 0 to 15 decimal places.
Input mask	Text, Number, Currency and Date/Time	Uses special characters to show the type of input allowed, and whether or not input is required.
Caption	All data types	For display on forms and reports.
Default value	All except AutoNumber, Memo and OLE Object	Automatically completes field with default value. You can edit as necessary at data entry/edit.
Validation rule		Used to test that allowable data only is entered.
Validation text		Message to appear when validation rule is not met.
Required		Set to 'Yes' if data must be entered.
Indexed	Text, Number, Date/Time, Currency and AutoNumber	Indexing speeds up access to its data – fields that will be sorted or queried on should be indexed.

Designing the table

Basic steps

1 Type the first field name – 'CCID' (an ID code for the contact person).

2 Press **[Tab]** to move to the Data Type column.

3 Click the drop-down arrow and select a data type – **AutoNumber**.

4 Press **[Tab]** twice to take you to the **Field Name** column for the next field. Enter 'Title' as the name.

5 Press **[Tab]** and set the data type to **Text**.

6 Press **[F6]** to move to the **Properties** pane.

7 Delete the 50 in the field size (the default value) and enter 10.

8 Press **[F6]** to return to the upper pane.

9 Repeat steps 2–8 for the other fields.

Once you have created your new table in Design view, the Table Design window is displayed. The window has two panes.

◆ The upper pane is where you specify the field name and data type. Both of these are essential for each field.

◆ The lower pane is where you specify the properties.

Initially, the upper pane looks like a small empty datasheet, and the lower pane is blank (the properties appear automatically when you add a field name and data type in the upper pane).

Current field indicator

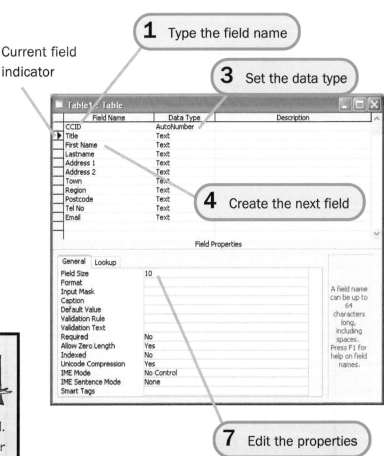

1 Type the field name

3 Set the data type

4 Create the next field

7 Edit the properties

Take note

The Description field is optional. Anything typed here will appear on the Status Bar when you are entering data.

Setting the primary key

The primary key is the field in your table that will contain a unique value in each record.

Each person on our list will have a unique code CCID (for Christmas Card ID!) - so this will be the primary key for the Name and Address table.

Basic steps

1 Put the insertion point anywhere within the CCID field in the upper pane.

2 Click the **Primary Key** tool on the Table Design toolbar.

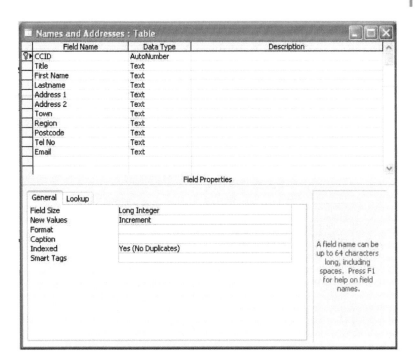

Take note

The primary key status can be switched on or off by clicking the Primary Key tool 🔑 when the insertion point is within the field (in the upper pane).

Take note

You can also use Text or Number fields for primary keys. If you do this, set the Index property to No Duplicates Allowed for the field – then Access will not accept a duplicate value in this field during data entry.

Save and close

- **Save**

1 Click the **Save** tool on the Table Design toolbar.

2 Give the table a meaningful name.

3 Click **OK**.

- **Close the window**

4 Click ☒ at the top right of the Table Design window to close it.

- **Close the file**

5 Click ☒ at the top right of the Database window to close it.

Save the table design

You should save the table design at this stage.

Close the Table Design window

That is the structure of our table complete. We will discuss data entry later – so close the table design window.

Close the database file

As this is the only table in the database, close the database file.

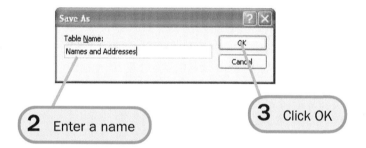

2 Enter a name

3 Click OK

5 Close the database window

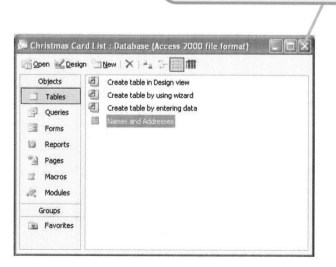

Take note

You must always save the table design once you have created or edited it.

Multi-table databases

We will now work through setting up the database file described in Chapter 1. The database file should be called 'Book Shop' and it will contain these two tables: 'Book' and 'Publisher'.

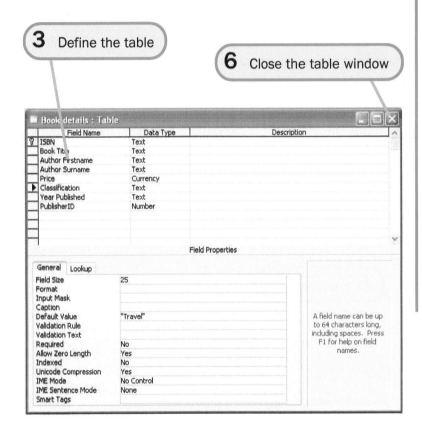

3 Define the table

6 Close the table window

Basic steps

1 Create a database file called 'Book Shop'.

2 Create a table in Design view for the Book details.

3 Enter the table structure – field names, data types and properties.

4 Set the primary key.

5 Save the table design - call it 'Book details'.

6 Close the Table Design window.

7 Repeat steps 2–6 for the Publisher table (call it 'Publisher').

8 Close the Book Shop database file.

Take note

The ISBN (International Standard Book Number) appears on the back of each book e.g. 0-7506-4182-7.

Take note

When you specify a default value for a field, the field is automatically completed with that value for each new record. Simply replace the default text with the text required as necessary.

Book table

Field name	Data type	Properties	Notes
ISBN	Text	Field size = 14	Primary key
Book title	Text	Field size = 30	
Author firstname	Text	Field size = 15	
Author surname	Text	Field size = 20	Indexed
Price	Currency	2 decimal places	
Classification	Text	Field size = 25; Default = Travel	
Year published	Text	Field size = 4	
PublisherID	Number	Long Integer	

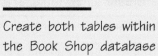

Take note

Create both tables within the Book Shop database file.

Publisher table

Field name	Data type	Properties	Notes
PublisherID	AutoNumber		Primary key
Publisher name	Text	Field size = 30	
Contact person	Text	Field size = 35	
Address 1	Text	Field size = 25	
Address 2	Text	Field size = 25	
Town	Text	Field size = 20	
Region	Text	Field size = 20	
Country	Text	Field size = 20	
Postcode	Text	Field size = 12	
Tel no	Text	Field size = 18	
Email	Text	Field size = 25	

Take note

You will find out how to create a relationship between these tables in Chapter 3.

Data entry will be discussed in Chapter 4.

Exercises

DVD Store database

You work in a DVD store, and have been given the task of setting up a database to record details of the DVDs that you stock, the members and the loans made by members. Set up the structure for the database following the guidelines below.

1 Create a new database – call it 'DVD Store'.

DVD Stock table

2 Create a new table, and enter the following table structure

Field name	Data type	Properties
DVDID	AutoNumber	Primary key
Title	Text	Size = 25, Indexed (Duplicates OK)
Classification	Text	Size = 20, Indexed (Duplicates OK)
Year released	Text	Size = 4
Company	Text	Size = 30, Indexed (Duplicates OK)

3 Save your table as 'DVD stock' and close it.

Member table

4 Create a new table, and enter the following table structure

Field name	Data type	Properties
MemberID	AutoNumber	Primary key
Title	Text	Field size = 6
First name/Initial	Text	Field size = 20
Surname	Text	Field size = 25, Indexed (Duplicates OK)
Address	Text	Field size = 30
Town	Text	Field size = 20, Indexed (Duplicates OK), Default value = Edinburgh
Postcode	Text	Field size = 10, Default value = EH
Region	Text	Field size = 20, Indexed (Duplicates OK), Default value = Lothian
Tel no	Text	Field size = 20, Default value = "0131"
Email	Text	Field size = 25
Child member	Yes/No	

5 Save your table as 'Members' and close it.

Take note

Indexing speeds up access to the data in that field. Fields that will be sorted or queried should be indexed.

Indexed (Duplicates OK) means that the field can contain the same value in more than one record, e.g. Town or Surname field.

Indexed (No Duplicates) ensures that each record has a unique value in the field — useful for primary key fields.

Loan table

6   Create a new table, and enter the following table structure

Field name	Data type	Properties
LoanID	AutoNumber	
MemberID	Number	Long integer
DVDID	Number	Long integer
Return date	Date/Time	Short date
Rental price	Currency	
Paid	Yes/No	

7   Save your table as 'Loans' and close it.

8   Close the DVD Store database file.

Personnel database

You have been given the task of setting up a Personnel database to record details of the staff who work for your company and the course bookings that are made on company training courses. Set up the structure for the database following the guidelines below.

1   Create a new database – call it 'Personnel'.

Staff table

2   Create a new table, and enter the following table structure

Field name	Data type	Properties
Staff code	Text	Field size = 6, Primary key
Title	Text	Field size = 10
First name	Text	Field size = 25
Surname	Text	Field size = 20
Start Date	Date/Time	Short date format
Salary	Currency	0 decimal places
		Validation rule <100000
Date of birth	Date/Time	Short date format
Job Title	Text	Field size = 25

Tip

When entering the Telephone number default value, use quotation marks, e.g. "0131" so Access accepts it as a text rather than a number. If Access thinks it is a number, it will drop the leading O.

3   Save your table as 'Staff' and close it.

Courses table

4   Create a new table, and enter the following table structure

Field name	Data type	Properties
Course ID	Text	Primary key, Field size = 10
Course title	Text	Field size = 25

5   Save your table as 'Courses' and close it.

Course Booking table

6   Create a new table, and enter the following table structure

Field name	Data type	Properties
Booking ID	Autonumber	Primary key
Course ID	Text	Field size = 10
Staff code	Text	Field size = 6
Course start date	Date/Time	Short Date

7   Save your table as 'Course booking' and close it.

8   Close the Personnel database file.

Take note

Data entered into a field that has a validation rule set will be checked against the rule. An error message will be displayed if the rule is broken.

Take note

You will find out how to create relationships between these tables so that the data from all can be used, in Chapter 3.

3 Relationships

Relationships

Now that the tables have been set up, we can establish the relationships between them. Once the relationships have been established you will be able to bring together information from several tables into queries, forms and reports.

Open the Book Shop database created in Chapter 2.

◆ We will create a relationship between the Book table and the Publisher table.

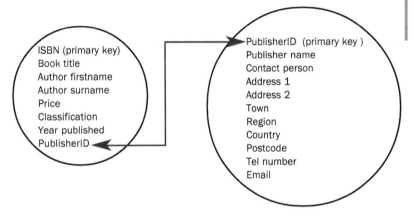

Relationships can be created, edited and deleted in the Relationships window.

Basic steps

1 From the Database window, click the **Relationships** tool .

or

2 Choose **Relationships** from the **Tools** menu.

The **Relationships** window and the **Show Table** dialog box are displayed.

Take note

You should close all tables and return to the Database window before you open the Relationships window.

Basic steps

1 If necessary, click the **Show Table** tool in the **Relationships** window to display the **Show Table** dialog box.

2 Select the tables to add to the Relationships window – to add several at once, click on the first, hold down [**Ctrl**] and click on the others.

3 Click [Add] to add them to the Relationships window.

4 If you add a table by mistake, click on it in the Relationships window and press [**Delete**].

5 Click [Close].

The tables that you wish to create relationships between must be displayed in the Relationships window. You can add tables and queries to the Relationships window from the Show Table dialog box. The dialog box is shown automatically the first time you open the Relationships window in a database file.

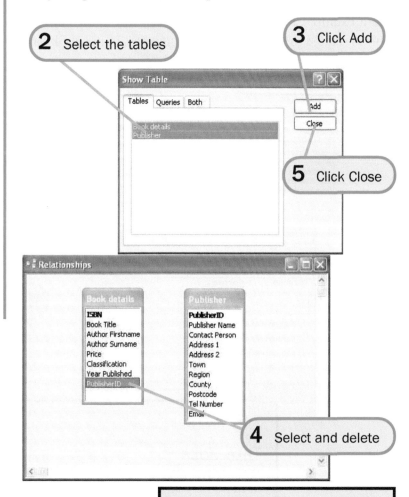

Take note

To display the design of any table in the Relationships window – right-click on the table and choose Table Design. When you close Design View, you are returned to the Relationships window.

Take note

You can move and resize the field lists within the Relationships window.

Making relationships

You must now make the relationships between the tables. A relationship will normally be between the primary key field in one table and its corresponding field in the related table (there called a foreign key - one that refers to the primary key of a different table).

In our example: Publisher ID, the primary key in the Publisher table is related to Publisher ID, a foreign key, in the Book table.

1. In the Relationships window, display the field in one table that will be related to the matching field in another, e.g. Publisher ID.

2. Drag the field name from the first table, and drop it on the related field in the other.

3. At the **Edit Relationship** dialog box select **Enforce Referential Integrity**.

4. Click Create.

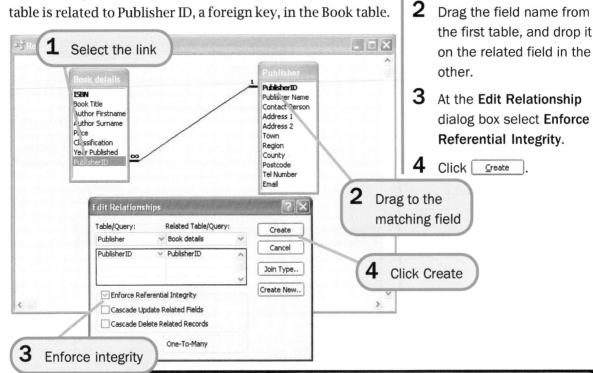

Take note

Related fields do not have to have the same name, but it makes things simpler if they do. They must normally, however, have the same data type. A text field can be related to another text field, but not to a number field. A number field can be related to a number field provided the FieldSize settings are the same.

The exception is an AutoNumber field. You can match an AutoNumber with a Number field whose FieldSize is set to Long Integer.

Referential integrity

These are the rules that are followed to preserve the defined relationships between tables when you enter or delete records.

If you enforce referential integrity, Access prevents you from:

◆ Adding records to a related table when there is no associated record in the primary table

◆ Changing values in the primary table that would result in orphan (unconnected) records in a related table

◆ Deleting records from the primary table when there are matching related records in a related table.

Types of relationships

One-To-Many	One of the related fields is a primary key or has a unique index.
	This is the most common type or relationship. In these, a record in the Publisher table can have many matching records in the Book details table (many books may be supplied by the same publisher).
One-To-One	Both of the fields are primary keys or have unique indexes.
	In this relationship type, each record in the first table can have only one matching record in the second, and vice versa. One-to-one relationships are sometimes used to divide a table that has many fields, or to isolate some fields for security reasons. This type of relationship is not very common.
Indeterminate	Neither of the related fields are primary keys nor have unique indexes.
	A record in the first table can have many matching records in the second, and a record in the second can have several matching records in the first. This type of relationship is only possible by defining a third table (called a junction table) whose primary key consists of two fields – the foreign keys from both the first and second tables. A many-to-many relationship is really two one-to-many relationships with a third table.

Editing and deleting

You can edit and/or delete relationships in the Relationships window.

- **Edit a relationship**
- **1** Double-click on the Join line connecting the tables.
- **2** Make the alterations in the **Edit Relationships** dialog box.
- **3** Click [OK].
- **Delete a relationship**
- **4** Click the Join line.
- **5** Press **[Delete]** and click [Yes] to confirm at the prompt.

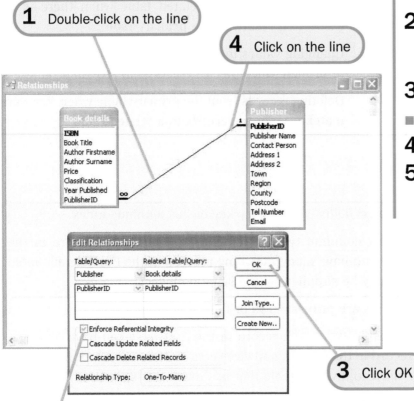

1 Double-click on the line

4 Click on the line

3 Click OK

2 Edit the relationship

Take note

Ensure that the tables are related as required, and save the relationship lay-out – click the [□] tool on the Relationships toolbar in the Relationships window.

Basic steps

1 Display the **Relationships** window.

2 Open the **File** menu and choose **Print Relationships...**

A preview of the printout will appear.

3 Click 🖨 on the **Print Preview** toolbar to print.

4 Click ❌ to close the Preview window.

5 If you wish to save the report, click [Yes] at the prompt.

6 Accept or edit the report name.

7 Click [OK]. It will be listed under **Reports** in the Database window.

8 Close the Book Shop database file.

Printing

You can easily take a printout of the relationships between your tables for reference purposes.

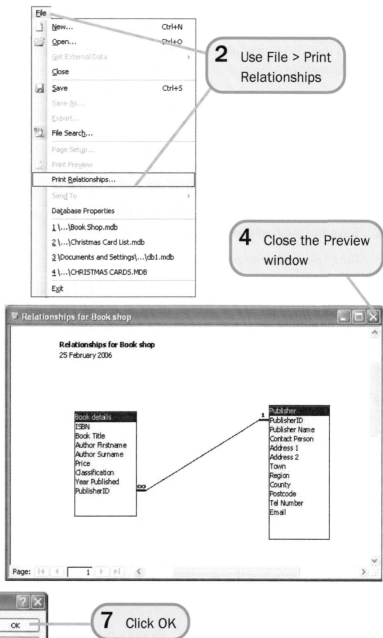

2 Use File > Print Relationships

4 Close the Preview window

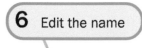

6 Edit the name

7 Click OK

Exercises

DVD Store database

1 Open the DVD Store database file.

2 Display the Relationships window.

3 Add the DVD Stock, Members and Loan tables to the Relationship window.

4 Create a relationship between the DVDID field in the Stock table and DVDID field in the Loan table. Enforce referential integrity on the relationship.

5 Create a relationship between the MemberID field in the Members table and MemberID field in the Loans table. Enforce referential integrity on the relationship.

6 Save the relationships layout.

7 Print the relationships report.

8 Close the Relationships window and the DVD Store file.

Personnel database

1 Open the Personnel database file.

2   Display the Relationships window.

3 Add the Staff and Course Bookings tables to the Relationships window.

4 Create a relationship between the Staff code field in the Staff table and Staff code field in the Course booking table. Enforce referential integrity on the relationship.

5 Create a relationship between the CourseID field in the Courses table and CourseID in the Course booking table. Enforce referential integrity on the relationship.

6 Save the relationships layout.

7 Print the relationships report.

8 Close the Relationships window and the Personnel database file.

4 Data entry and edit

Using Datasheet view

Once you have set up the structure of your table(s) and set the relationships, the next stage is data entry. The table should be displayed in Datasheet view rather than Design view for this. In Datasheet view, each column of the table is a field and each row is a record.

Try entering some records into your table using your Christmas Card List database.

Basic steps

1 Open the database file.

2 Display the **Tables** in the Database window.

3 Double-click on a table to open it in Datasheet view.

or

4 Select it and click on the Database window toolbar.

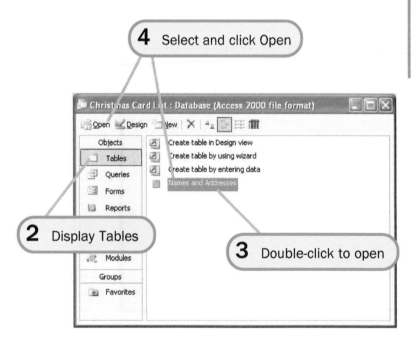

4 Select and click Open

2 Display Tables

3 Double-click to open

Take note

To open a table in Design view, select it in the Database window and click on ⫧Design the Database window toolbar.

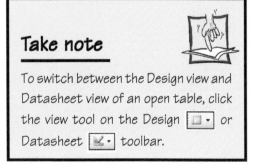

Take note

To switch between the Design view and Datasheet view of an open table, click the view tool on the Design ▥▾ or Datasheet ⫧▾ toolbar.

Entering data

Basic steps

1 Type the data required into the first field.

2 Press **[Tab]** to take you forward to the next field.

or

Press **[Shift]–[Tab]** to take you back to the previous field.

3 At the end of a record, press **[Tab]** to take you to the first field in the next record.

Each record is saved automatically when you move onto the next.

4 Close the table when finished.

Entering data is easy. If you have used tables in Word, or Excel, the method is very similar.

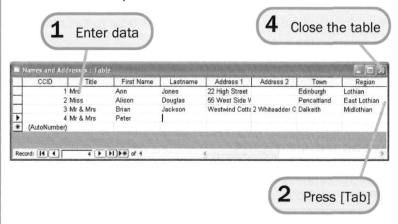

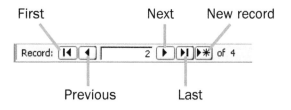

Moving around your datasheet

In addition to using the **[Tab]** and **[Shift]–[Tab]** to move between fields, you can:

◆ Point and click with the mouse to go to any field (using the scroll bars as necessary to bring the field into view).

◆ Use the Navigation Bar.

◆ Go to a specific record number - press **[F5]**, key in the record number and press **[Enter]**.

Take note

The value in the CCID field will be generated automatically as it is an AutoNumber field.

45

Editing

You can edit data at any time. If you move onto a field using [**Tab**] or [**Shift**]–[**Tab**] the data in it is selected. You can then:

◆ Replace the current contents. Just type in the new data while the old is highlighted

◆ Edit the data. Press [**F2**] to deselect the text, then position the insertion point using the Arrow keys

◆ Erase the contents. Press [**Delete**].

Keyboard shortcuts

[PgUp]	Up a screen	[Ctrl]-[PgUp]	Left a screen width
[↑]	Current field, previous record	[Ctrl]-[↑]	Current field, first record
[PgDn]	Down a screen	[Ctrl]-[PgDn]	Right a screen width
[↓]	Current field, next record	[Ctrl]-[↓]	Current field, last record
[Home]	First field, current record	[Ctrl]-[Home]	First field, first record
[End]	Last field, current record	[Ctrl]-[End]	Last field, last record

Adjusting column widths

When you create an Access table, the fields/columns are displayed at a standard width, regardless of the Field Size specified in the Properties panel in Design view. You can easily adjust the column width by dragging the vertical bar between the field names at the top of each field.

If you adjust the column widths in Datasheet view, you will be prompted to save the layout changes when you close the table. Click [Yes] or [No], depending on whether you wish to save the changes or not.

Take note

If you have made an error in field size when setting up your tables, go into Design view for the table and update the field size, save the table, then return to Datasheet view to continue entering your data.

Basic steps

Add and delete records

- **Add a new record**

1 Click the **New Record** tool on the Standard toolbar, or ▶✱ on the navigation bar at the bottom right of the table. The insertion point will be placed in the first field of the next empty row in your table.

2 Enter your record details.

- **Delete a record**

3 Place the insertion point anywhere in the record.

4 Click the **Delete Record** tool ⊠ on the Standard toolbar.

5 Respond to the prompt. Click [Yes] to go ahead with the deletion, or [No] if you have changed your mind.

◆ If you have the Christmas Card List database file open, close it now.

Each time you add a record, it is added to the end of the list of records in your table. As records can easily be sorted into any order, this initial placing is not that important.

You can quickly jump to the end of your table, ready to add the next record, from anywhere in your list of records.

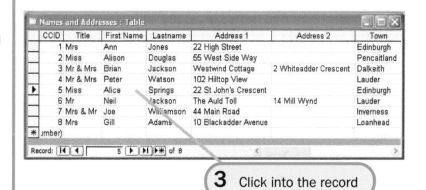

3 Click into the record

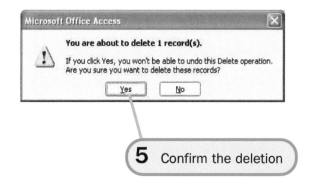

5 Confirm the deletion

Take note

To delete a table, select it in the Database window and press the [Delete] key.

Take note

Once you have deleted a record, you cannot undo the delete. If you delete your record in error, you will need to type it in again.

Adjusting the design

If you discover any errors in your table design at the data entry stage, you can go back to Design view and adjust the table structure. You can add and delete fields or edit any of the other attributes e.g. field name, data type, field properties, of your tables.

◆ You must be in Design view to edit the structure.

Take note

If you try to delete or change the primary key status of a field that is part of a relationship, you will be prompted to delete the relationship first. You must close your table and return to the Relationships window to do this. Remember to save your changes, and then return to Table Design to adjust the table structure.

Tip

You can edit a field's name or properties at any time. just click into the field and make the changes in the upper or lower pane.

1 Select your table it in the Database window and click to open it in Design view.

or

2 If the table is open in Datasheet view, click the **View** tool on the Datasheet toolbar.

■ **Add a field at the end**

3 Go to the first empty row in the upper pane and enter the field definition.

■ **Add a field within the list**

4 Click in the field that will go below the new one (in the upper pane).

5 Click the **Insert Row** tool on the Table Design toolbar.

6 Enter the field definition.

■ **Delete a field**

7 Click in the field.

8 Click the **Delete Row** tool on the Table Design toolbar.

Data and related tables

1 Open the Book Shop database.

2 Open the Publisher table in Datasheet view.

3 Type in the Publisher records.

4 Close the table.

5 Open the Book details table in Datasheet view.

6 Type in the Book records.

7 Close the table.

8 Close the Book Shop database file.

When entering data into a database where there are related tables, and referential integrity has been enforced, you must add each record to the table at the ONE side of the relationship before you add related records to the MANY side.

There is a one-to-many relationship between the Publisher table and the Book details table in the Book Shop database (one publisher may supply us with many books). When you add records to the Book details table, the PublisherID field must be completed so that the publisher can be identified. Access will check that the value you type into the PublisherID field in the Book details table has a matching value in the PublisherID field in the Publisher table. If a match isn't found, an error message will be displayed and you cannot complete the record.

Delete the County field from the Publisher table

PUBLISHER TABLE

ID	Name	Contact	Address 1	Address 2	Town	Region	County	Postcode	Tel Num	Email
1	Elsevier	Jack Smith	The Boulevard	Langford Lane	Oxford			OX5 1GB	01352 111 4444	JackS@elsevier.co.uk
2	Puffin Magic	Alice Williamson	7 Queen Street		Edinburgh	Lothian		EH34 1ZZ	0131 999 1111	Awill@puffin.co.uk
3	Arrows Publications	George Black	Randall House	1 Cavalier Bridge Road	London			RM10 2SA	020 8443 9000	Gblack@arrows.co.uk
4	Wayward Lock Ltd	Nikki Madson	18 Clifftop Street		London			WC1H 3PP	020 7444 2222	Nmadson@wayward.co.uk
5	Harry Cousin Ltd	Paul Thomson	10-23 Frosty Road		Inverness	Highland		IV4 2AA	01463 222 4444	PaulT@HarryC.co.uk

Take note

If you try to add a duplicate primary key value, you will be told that this cannot be done. Edit the primary key field entry to clear the error.

BOOK DETAILS

ISBN	Book title	Author firstname	Author surname	Price £	Classification	Year published	PublisherID
0 1122 3344 5	Easy Internet	Morris	McNally	11.99	Computing	2003	2
0 1402 3832 1	In & Out Stories	Jack	Simpson	7.50	Children's fiction	1997	2
0 1403 7022 6	Castaways	Maggie	Anderson	11.99	Travel	1999	1
0 3320 6666 1	Christmas Destinations	Davina	Cousins	14.99	Travel	2005	1
0 3355 2211 8	Garden Shrubs	Alice	Borthwick	9.99	Gardening	2004	1
0 3451 2244 3	Campfire Cooking	Jim	Peterson	12.00	Cooking	2002	3
0 4231 4422 5	West Highland Way	Andrew	McLeod	18.99	Travel	2005	2
0 4422 1212 5	Cycling in Holland	Toni	Wilson	14.75	Travel	2004	4
0 4422 3311 2	Bits and Bytes	Colin	Donaldson	12.99	Computing	2003	3
0 4433 2233 4	Crazy Comets	William	Custard	20.00	Science	2005	5
0 4466 8833 1	Changing Skies	Martin	Andrews	16.99	Travel	2002	3
0 5532 7722 1	Bread and Biscuits	Caroline	Andrews	14.99	Cooking	2002	1
0 5555 2233 4	Ballet Music from Russia	Stephen	Black	15.99	Music	2001	4
0 6622 9944 1	Giant World Atlas	Toni	Wilson	12.99	Travel	2001	2
0 7733 2200 2	Jazz & Blues Highlights	Gordon	French	12.75	Music	2004	5
0 7744 6664 2	Guitar Classics	Frank	Powell	14.99	Music	2002	3
0 7755 2211 3	Little Bear at Home	Amanda	Hastings	7.99	Children's fiction	2005	2
0 7755 5511 3	Little Bear on holiday	Amanda	Hastings	7.99	Children's fiction	2005	2
0 9922 3322 1	The Western Isles	Tracy	Littlejohn	14.99	Travel	2003	5
0 9933 2255 6	Outdoor Adventures	Francis	Donaldson	9.75	Travel	2005	4

Take note

If you enter PublisherID data in the Book details table, that does not exist in the Publisher table, this message appears:

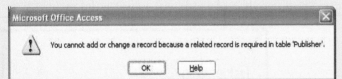

Access will not accept a PublisherID in the Book details table that has no corresponding value in the Publisher table.

Exercises

1 Open the **DVD Store database**

2 Set the Title field size to 60, then enter the following records into the DVD Stock table.

DVDID	Title	Classification	Year released	Director
1	Batman Begins	12A	2005	Christopher Nolan
2	Charlie and the Chocolate Factory	PG	2005	Tim Burton
3	Concert for George	PG	2003	David DeLand
4	Dreamcatcher	15	2004	Lawrence Kasdan
5	Fahrenheit 9/11	15	2004	Michael Moore
6	The Good, the Bad, and the Ugly: Special Edition	18	2004	Sergio Leone
7	Harry Potter and the Prisoner of Azkaban	PG	2004	Alfonso Cuaron
8	The Lord of the Rings: The Return of the King	12A	2004	Peter Jackson
9	Shrek 2	U	2004	Andrew Adamson
10	Wallace and Gromit: Curse of the Were-Rabbit	U	2006	Nick Park

3 You could add other DVDs try **http://www.futuremovies.co.uk/review.asp** for ideas.

4 Complete the Members table with their contact details. Add more if you wish.

ID	Title	First name	Surname	Address 1	Address 2	Town	Postcode	Region	Tel no	Email	Child member
1	Mrs	Amanda	Shakespeare	22 St Stephen Street		Edinburgh	EH6 1ZZ	Lothian	0131 333 5555		No
2	Mr	Peter	Watson	14 Circus Place Lane		Edinburgh	EH8 2PP	Lothian	0131 555 1111	peterw@ yahoo.co.uk	No
3	Mr	Alexander	Borthwick	1st flat left	22 Eyre Place	Edinburgh	EH14 1QQ	Lothian	0131 444 2233	alex@btinternet .co.uk	No
4	Miss	Megan	Halcroft	The Elms	33 Hamilton Place	Edinburgh	EH23 2RT	Lothian	0131 443 1000	meganh@quista .co.uk	Yes
5	Mrs	Sarah	Peterson	48 St Andrew's Close		Edinburgh	EH3 2SG	Lothian	0131 444 9987		No
6	Mr	Jack	Thomson	31a Castle Terrace		Edinburgh	EH2 4TT	Lothian	0131 533 3322	spiderman@ yahoo.co.uk	Yes
7	Mrs	Trish	Blackwood	99 Queen's Court		Edinburgh	EH3 7PR	Lothian	0131 338 4455	tblackwood@ hotmail.co.uk	No
8	Mrs	Emma	McLean	44 Hill Street		Dalkeith	EH34 1ZZ	Lothian	0131 775 4422	emmab@virgin .net	No
9	Mr	Fred	Watson	12 Castle Court		Edinburgh	EH2 6RT	Lothian	0131 334 2121		No
10	Mr	Thomas	Clelland	32 Marchmont Street		Edinburgh	EH9 1XX	Lothian	0131 554 6603	thomclelland@ yahoo.co.uk	Yes

5   Open the Loans table and enter details of the loans.

LoanID	DVDID	MemberID	Return Date	Rental Price	Paid
1	2	5	01/06/2006	£3.00	Yes
2	3	10	01/06/2006	£3.00	Yes
3	6	2	01/06/2006	£3.50	No
4	4	9	01/06/2006	£3.00	Yes
5	2	7	04/06/2006	£3.00	Yes
6	3	5	04/06/2006	£3.00	Yes
7	6	7	05/06/2006	£3.50	Yes
8	9	1	05/06/2006	£2.50	No
9	1	5	08/06/2006	£3.00	Yes
10	6	4	08/06/2006	£3.50	Yes
11	7	8	08/06/2006	£3.00	Yes
12	9	6	10/06/2006	£3.00	Yes

6   Add more records if you want, and close the DVD Store file.

7   Open the Personnel database file

8   Add the records to the Staff table.

StaffID	Title	Firstname	Surname	Start Date	Salary	Date of Birth	Job Title
MS0001	Mrs	Margaret	Simpson	03/05/2004	£26,500.00	04/06/1962	Sales Administrator
RB0001	Mr	Robert	Burns	06/04/1996	£32,000.00	14/03/1958	Account Manager
WS0001	Mr	William	Stewart	26/02/2001	£18,900.00	30/10/1985	Web Designer
MS0002	Mrs	Monica	Smart	16/11/2005	£29,500.00	25/01/1978	Editor
AL0001	Mr	Andrew	Lipson	18/09/2003	£22,000.00	01/09/1981	Chef

9   And the records to the Courses table.

CourseID	Course title
HASAW	Health and Safety at Work
DPA	Data Protection Act
SEC	Security
BITS	Basic IT Skills

10 And finally the Course booking table.

Booking ID	Staff code	Course ID	Course start date
1	MS0001	BITS	01/09/2006
2	MS0001	HASAW	01/10/2006
3	AL0001	DPA	03/09/2006
4	WS0001	BITS	01/09/2006
5	RB0001	BITS	01/09/2006
6	AL0001	HASAW	01/12/2006
7	WS0001	HASAW	01/12/2006
8	MS0002	DPA	03/09/2006
9	RB0001	DPA	04/11/2006
10	MS0002	BITS	01/12/2006

11 Close the Personnel database file.

Take note

When entering data into the postcode and telephone number fields in the Members table, tab to the field, press [F2] – this will place the insertion point at the end of the field, after the default data. Complete the field.

Take note

The tables at the ONE side of a one-to-many relationship were completed before data was entered into the table at the MANY side of the relationship.

5 Forms

Creating Forms

Forms allow you to customise your screen for input and editing purposes. Although data entry and edit is often done directly onto the table datasheet, forms are very useful as they allow for simpler and more accurate data entry.

Forms can be created in a number of ways – using the AutoForm feature, a Form Wizard, or directly into the Design view of the form.

Any forms that you save will be listed under Forms in the database window.

Autoform

A simple form can be created quickly using the **AutoForm** feature. Try creating an AutoForm for the table in your Christmas Card List database

1 Open your database.

2 Display the tables in the Database window.

3 Select the table – Names and Addresses – that you want to create a form for.

4 Click the **AutoForm** tool in the **New Object** list.

A simple form will be displayed, showing the first record in your table.

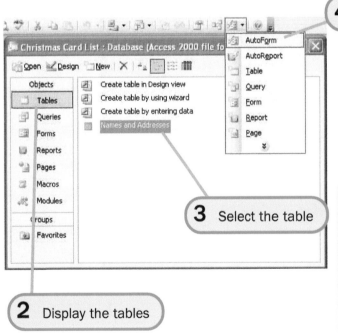

4 Click AutoForm

3 Select the table

2 Display the tables

The form has no great design frills, but it does the job

54

Working in Form view

The techniques that you use in Datasheet view also apply in Form view:

◆ To add records to your form, click the **New Record** tool on the Standard toolbar or ▶✳ on the Navigation Bar at the bottom of the form.

◆ To move from field to field within each record, press **[Tab]** to move forwards, or **[Shift]**-**[Tab]** to move backwards. Alternatively, click in the field you wish to work in.

◆ To move from one record to another, use the Navigation Bar at the bottom of the form.

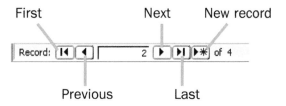

◆ To delete a record, display it and then click the Delete tool ▶✕ on the Standard toolbar.

◆ Add another three or four records using the form that you have created.

Save and close a form

If you wish to keep your form so that you can reuse it you must save it.

Basic steps

1 Click the **Save** tool on the Form View toolbar.

2 Give the form a meaning-ful name.

3 Click [OK].

4 Close your form.

You will find your form listed in the Forms area in the Database window.

5 Close the Christmas Card List database file.

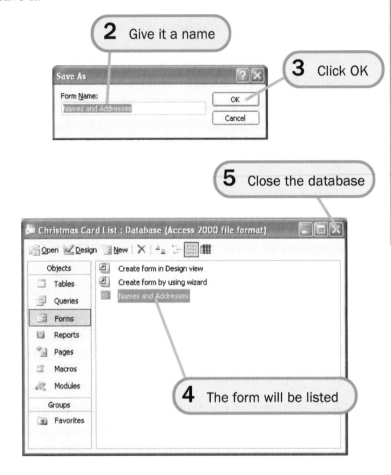

2 Give it a name

3 Click OK

5 Close the database

4 The form will be listed

Take note

When you add or edit records through a form, the actual data is stored in the underlying Table, not in the Form. The data will still be saved, even if you do not save the Form.

Take note

To delete a form, select it in the Database window and press [Delete].

Tip

To open a form that has been saved, double-click on it in the Database window.

56

Forms and related tables

1 Open the Book Shop database.

2 Create an AutoForm for the Book details table.

3 Add two or three new books using the form.

4 Save and close the form.

5 Create an AutoForm for the Publisher table.

6 Add a new publisher.

7 Add two new books for that publisher.

8 Save and close the form.

9 Close the Book Shop database file.

Take note

Once you have closed your forms, open the tables in Datasheet view – your new and updated records will be there.

Use AutoForm again, this time on the Book Shop database.

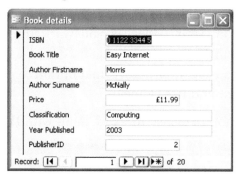

The Publisher table is at the one side of a one-to-many relationship. When you create an AutoForm, the data from the Publisher table is in the top of the form, and the data from the Book details table are listed in the lower part, in a subform.

If you look at the Navigation bar area, you will notice two sets of buttons. The lower set belongs to the Publisher table, the upper set to the Book details table.

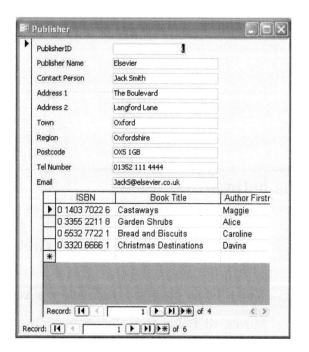

Form Wizard

As an alternative to using AutoForm to create a form, you could create a form using the Form Wizard. You can select specific fields from your tables as you work through the wizard (rather than having all fields as is the case with the AutoForm) and also apply an AutoFormat option to give your form more interest and user appeal.

Open the Book Shop database to experiment with this.

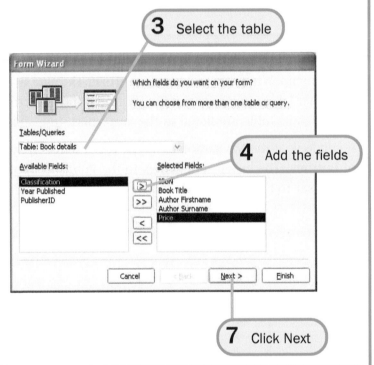

3 Select the table

4 Add the fields

7 Click Next

The buttons

[>]	Moves a field from **Available Fields** to **Selected Fields**
[>>]	Moves all fields from **Available Fields** to **Selected Fields**
[<]	Moves a field from **Selected Fields** to **Available Fields**
[<<]	Moves all fields from **Selected Fields** to **Available Fields**

Basic steps

- **Selecting the fields**

1 Go to the Forms area in the Database window.

2 Double click
 [≥] Create form by using wizard .

3 Select the Table that you want to create a form for – Publishers.

 The fields in the table will be displayed in the **Available Fields** list

4 Add to the **Selected Fields** list those fields that will appear on the form – PublisherID, Name, Contact Person, Tel Number and Email.

5 Select another table from the Tables/Queries list if necessary – Book details in this case.

6 Add the fields you require from it - ISBN, Book Title, Author Firstname, Author Surname, Price.

7 Click Next > .

Basic steps

- **Viewing your data**

1 Choose the table that you wish to view your data by, e.g. Publisher or Book details – choose Publisher.

2 Select whether you wish to create a form with subform(s) or linked forms.

3 Click [Next >].

- **Layout**

4 Select the layout that you want to use – choose either Tabular or Datasheet.

5 Click [Next >].

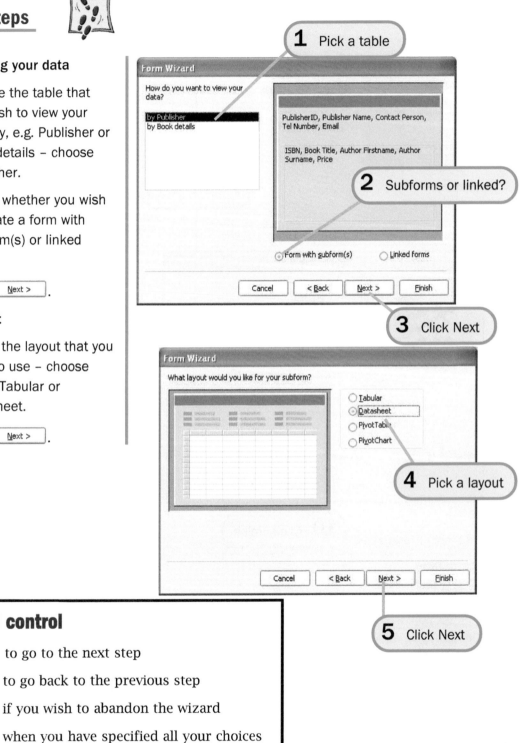

1 Pick a table

2 Subforms or linked?

3 Click Next

4 Pick a layout

5 Click Next

Wizard control

[Next >]	to go to the next step
[< Back]	to go back to the previous step
[Cancel]	if you wish to abandon the wizard
[Finish]	when you have specified all your choices

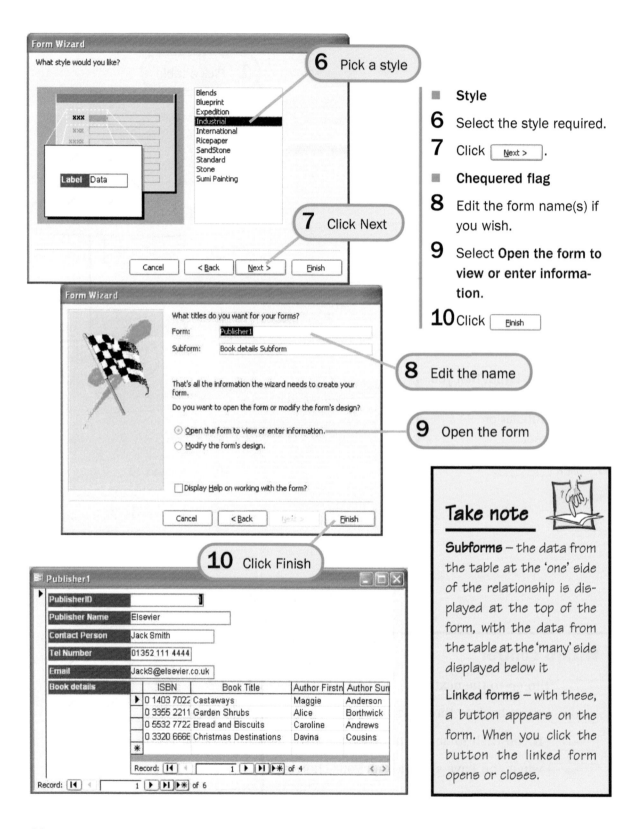

Form Wizard

What style would you like?

6 Pick a style

Blends
Blueprint
Expedition
Industrial
International
Ricepaper
SandStone
Standard
Stone
Sumi Painting

Label Data

7 Click Next

Cancel | < Back | Next > | Finish

Form Wizard

What titles do you want for your forms?

Form: Publisher1
Subform: Book details Subform

That's all the information the wizard needs to create your form.

Do you want to open the form or modify the form's design?

⊙ Open the form to view or enter information.
○ Modify the form's design.

☐ Display Help on working with the form?

Cancel | < Back | Next > | Finish

8 Edit the name

9 Open the form

10 Click Finish

Publisher1

PublisherID	1
Publisher Name	Elsevier
Contact Person	Jack Smith
Tel Number	01352 111 4444
Email	JackS@elsevier.co.uk

Book details

	ISBN	Book Title	Author Firstn	Author Sun
▶	0 1403 7022	Castaways	Maggie	Anderson
	0 3355 2211	Garden Shrubs	Alice	Borthwick
	0 5532 7722	Bread and Biscuits	Caroline	Andrews
	0 3320 6666	Christmas Destinations	Davina	Cousins
*				

Record: |◄ ◄ 1 ► ►| ►* of 4

Record: |◄ ◄ 1 ► ►| ►* of 6

■ **Style**

6 Select the style required.

7 Click [Next >].

■ **Chequered flag**

8 Edit the form name(s) if you wish.

9 Select **Open the form to view or enter information.**

10 Click [Finish]

Take note

Subforms – the data from the table at the 'one' side of the relationship is displayed at the top of the form, with the data from the table at the 'many' side displayed below it

Linked forms – with these, a button appears on the form. When you click the button the linked form opens or closes.

60

Basic steps

1 Go to the forms area in the Database window.

2 Select the Names and Addresses form.

3 Click **Design**.

4 Click [⚹] on the Form Design toolbar to toggle the display of the Toolbox.

5 Click [▭] to toggle the Field list display.

Take note

When a form is open, to move between Design view and Form view, click the View tool [◩▾] on the Form view toolbar, and the View tool [▤▾] on the Form Design toolbar.

The Design view of a form is useful for adding the finishing touches to it. You could add a heading or an instruction, format some text, insert a picture or add colour to a field.

It doesn't matter if you created the form using the AutoForm or the Wizard – you can still customise it in Design view.

Open the Christmas Card List database to experiment with Design view.

In Design view, the form is displayed on the design grid, and the field list (showing the fields that can be used on your form) and the toolbox are displayed.

The fields are displayed in the Detail area of the Form.

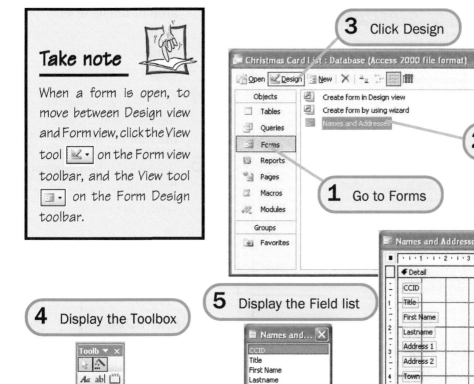

3 Click Design

2 Pick a form

1 Go to Forms

5 Display the Field list

4 Display the Toolbox

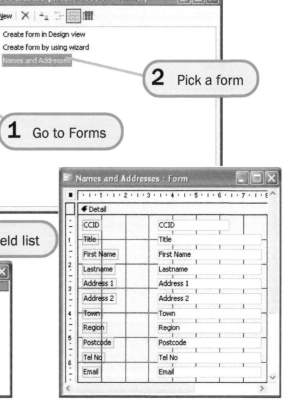

Form header and footer

The main form area is the Detail area – this is where the data from your table(s) is normally displayed.

Other main areas are the header and footer at the top and bottom of each form. They are often used for headings, instructions or descriptive text, a company logo, etc. – anything that you want displayed on each form.

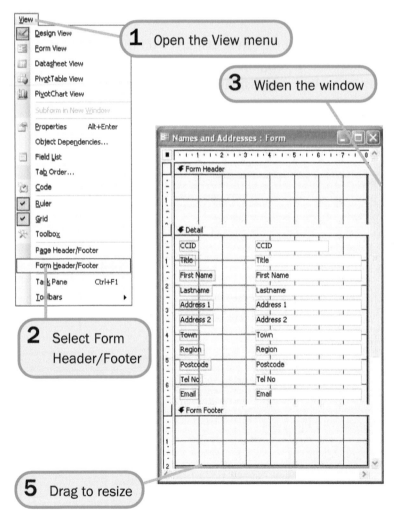

1 Open the View menu

3 Widen the window

2 Select Form Header/Footer

5 Drag to resize

- **Show the header/footer**

1 Open the **View** menu.

2 Click **Form Header/ Footer**.

The Form Header and Form Footer area will be displayed. You cannot have a header area without a footer area – it's both or neither.

3 You can resize any form area by dragging its border (resize the Design window so you see the edges of the form).

4 Drag the right edge of the form grid to adjust the width of the form.

5 Drag the bottom edge of the Header, Detail or Footer area to resize it.

Take note

In a form, the objects that you add are called controls. e.g. image control or label control.

Basic steps

- **Delete the field/control**

1 Select the field and press [Delete].

- **Resize the field/control**

2 Drag one of the handles – the mouse pointer should be a double-headed arrow.

- **Move the field/control**

3 Drag the edge – not a handle – the mouse pointer should be a hand shape.

Once you have added a field or a control to a form, you can easily delete, resize or move it.

You must select the field or control before you can do any of these - click on it. Handles appear in each corner and at the midpoint of the selected item.

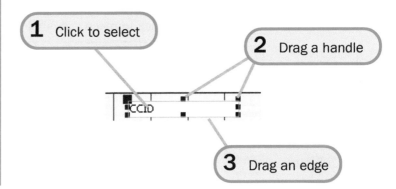

1 Click to select

2 Drag a handle

3 Drag an edge

Take note

To move the label or data part of a field independently, point to the top left handle of the side that you wish to move and click and drag – the cursor should be a pointing finger.

Take note

The fields that are displayed in the Detail area of the Form consist of two parts – the label (the field name), and the detail (where the actual data from the table will be displayed in the Form).

You can select (and work with) each part independently by clicking on it.

Labels

If you wish to add a heading, instructions or any other text that does not come from the data source (the list of fields that the form uses) you must enter it into a Label control.

Once you have entered your text, you can easily format it – increase the font size, make it bold, change the colour, etc.

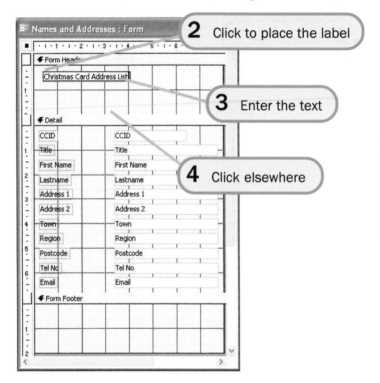

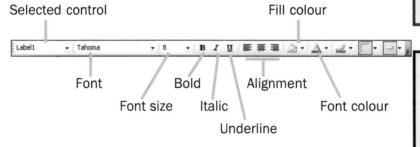

2 Click to place the label

3 Enter the text

4 Click elsewhere

Basic steps

1 Select the **Label** tool within the Toolbox.

2 Click on your form to indicate where you want to add the text, e.g. in the Form Header.

3 Type in your text.

4 Click outside the control, anywhere on your form.

■ **Format a control**

5 Click on the control once to select it.

6 Apply the formats using the Formatting (Form/Report) toolbar.

Formatting toolbar for forms and reports

Selected control

Fill colour

`Label1 ▾ Tahoma ▾ 8 ▾ B I U ≡ ≡ ≡ ⚏ ▾ A ▾ ⚿ ▾ ⬜ ▾ ⤶ ▾`

Font

Bold

Alignment

Font size

Italic

Font colour

Underline

Tip

To apply or change an AutoFormat choose Auto-Format from the Format menu. Select a format from the dialog box and click OK.

Take note

The label control does not resize itself if you increase the font size.

Basic steps

1 Select the **Image** control from the Toolbox.

2 Click where you want the picture to go on the form.

3 Locate the picture on your computer.

4 Select the picture and click [OK].

5 Resize and/or move the picture as necessary.

Images

You can add a picture or your company logo to a form using an Image control.

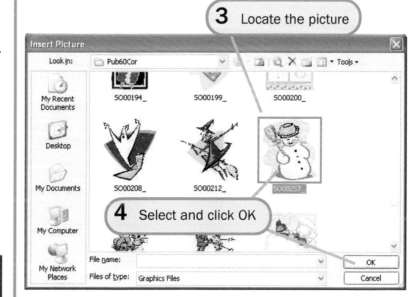

3 Locate the picture

4 Select and click OK

Tip

When working in Design view, move backward and forward between it and Form view as required to check how your form is developing.

Picture size mode

When you resize some pictures, they will be 'clipped'. The edges of the picture will disappear, and you will only see as much as fits within the control. Adjust the Size Mode property of the picture to get it to fit within the control.

Take note

The location of the clipart pictures may vary. Try C:\Program Files\Microsoft Office\Clipart.

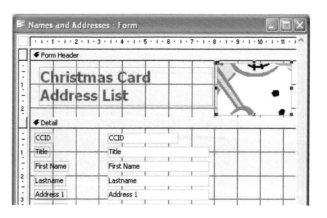

Resizing and moving

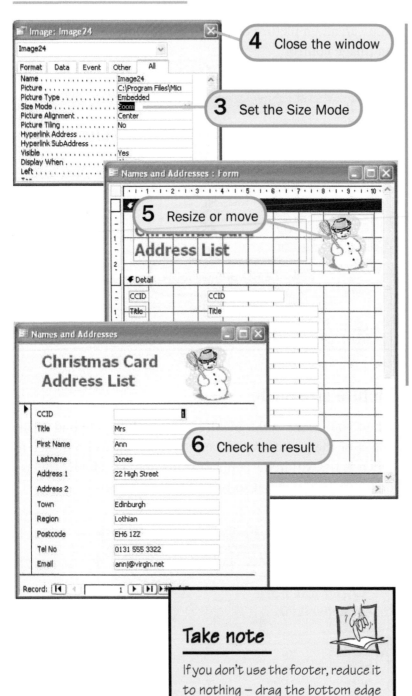

4 Close the window

3 Set the Size Mode

5 Resize or move

6 Check the result

1 Select the control.

2 Click the **Properties** tool on the Standard toolbar.

3 On the **All** tab, set the **Size Mode** property to **Zoom** or **Stretch** – whichever looks best.

4 Close the Image properties window.

5 Resize and/or move the image as required.

6 Return to Form view to view the final result.

◆ Close the Christmas Card List database file.

Tip

Although forms are normally used for data input and editing, you can print them (this can be useful if you are giving a completed form to someone to check). To print a form, view it, choose Print from the file menu, and specify Selected record(s) in the Print Range options in the dialog box.

Take note

If you don't use the footer, reduce it to nothing – drag the bottom edge of it up as far as it will go.

Exercises

Book shop database

Task 1

1 Open the Book Shop database.

2 Open the Book details form in Design view.

3 Display the form header/footer and add a label 'Books in stock' to the header. Format it size 14, bold and blue.

4 Insert an appropriate image in the header area. Resize, move and/or change the Size Mode property as necessary.

5 Add a label to the form footer and add your name. Format it as you wish.

6 Resize the form header/ footer area if necessary.

7 Save your form.

8 Display the form in Form view.

9 Print record 1 only and close your form.

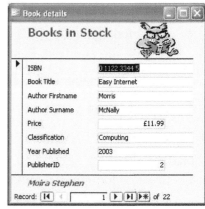

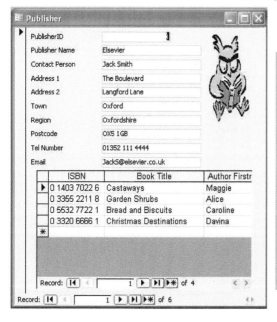

Task 2

1 Open the Publisher form in Design view.

2 Insert an appropriate image to the right of the Publisher details. Resize or move it as necessary.

3 Save your form.

4 Display the form in Form view.

5 Print record 2 only.

6 Close your form and close the Book Shop database file.

67

DVD store database

Task 1

1 Open the DVD Store database

2 Create a form for the DVD Stock table.

3 Add an image to the right of the DVD informa-tion. Set the size mode option to Zoom. Resize and move the image as necessary.

4 Format the DVD data field names as Comic Sans MS, blue and bold, then resize the fields to display the complete name if necessary.

5 Format the DVD data fields as Comic Sans MS.

6 Save the form.

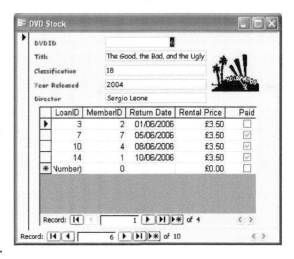

Task 2

1 Create a form for the Loans table.

2 Add a form header – DVD Loan Details, and format it size 14, red and bold. Resize the label as necessary.

3 Resize the header and reduce the footer to a minimum.

4 Save the form.

Task 3

1 Create a form for the Members table.

2 Add a form header – Member Information, and format it size 14, blue, bold and italics. Resize it so that all of the text is displayed.

3 Insert an image to the right of the header text. Set the Size Mode property for the image to either Zoom or Stretch. Move or resize the image to get a good fit in the header.

4 Resize the form header if necessary.

5 Reduce the size of the form footer to nothing.

6 Save the form and close the DVD Store data-base file.

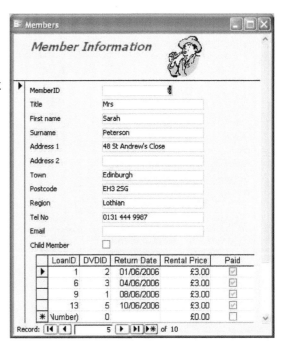

Personnel database

Task 1

1 Open the Personnel database file

2 Create a form for the Course booking table

3 Add a header – Course Booking Information. Format it as Comic Sans MS, size 15 and bold, then resize the label control to display all the text.

4 Resize the form header area to reduce any blank space.

5 Format the field names and data controls to use font Comic Sans MS. Resize them so that all text is displayed.

6 Add an image to the form footer then resize the footer to reduce the blank space.

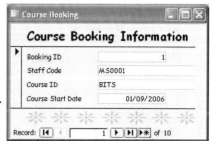

7 Save and close the form.

Task 2

1 Create a form for the Courses table.

2 Add a Form header – Course Information. Format it as Comic Sans MS, size 16, bold and blue.

3 Format the field name and data controls for the CourseID and Course Title to be Comic Sans MS.

4 Format the data area for these controls to be bold, with a pale blue background (Fill colour).

5 Adjust the sizes of the field name/data controls so that all text is displayed.

6 Save and close the form.

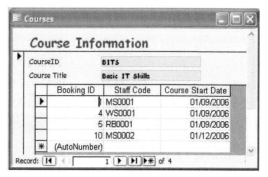

Task 3

1   Create a form for the Staff table.

2   Add a form header – Staff Training Data. Format it as Comic Sans MS, size 14, blue and bold.

3   Add an image to the right of the header text – set the Size Mode property to Zoom.

4   Format the field names and data controls to use font Comic Sans MS.

5   Format the data area of the control to have a pale blue fill colour, and bold text.

6   Add a footer – Compulsory Training Courses, and format it as Comic Sans MS, blue and italics.

7   Resize the header and footer areas to reduce any blank space.

8   Save and close the form.

9   Close the Personnel database file.

6 Datasheet view

Simple sort

The records in a table will normally appear in the order in which they were entered. You can easily sort the data in your table into ascending or descending order on any field.

Use the Names and Addresses table in your Christmas Card List database to experiment.

Basic steps

1 Open the table or form that you want to sort.

2 Click anywhere within the field that you wish to sort in order of.

3 Click the **Sort Ascending** or the **Sort Descending** tool – depending on the order required.

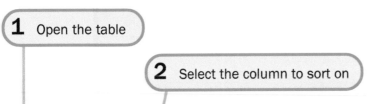

1 Open the table

2 Select the column to sort on

	CCID	Title	First Name	Lastname	Address 1	Address 2	Town	Region	Postcode
▶	8	Mrs	Gill	Adams	10 Blackadder Avenue		Loanhead	Midlothian	EH34 1ZZ
	2	Miss	Alison	Douglas	55 West Side Way		Pencaitland	East Lothian	EH44 2PP
	6	Mr	Neil	Jackson	The Auld Toll	14 Mill Wynd	Lauder	Borders	TD10 7ZZ
	3	Mr & Mrs	Brian	Jackson	Westwind Cottage	2 Whiteadder Crescent	Dalkeith	Midlothian	E22 5ZZ
	1	Mrs	Ann	Jones	22 High Street		Edinburgh	Lothian	EH6 1ZZ
	5	Miss	Alice	Springs	22 St John's Crescent		Edinburgh	Lothian	EH21 4WQ
	4	Mr & Mrs	Peter	Watson	102 Hilltop View		Lauder	Borders	TD10 ZZZ
	7	Mrs & Mr	Joe	Williamson	44 Main Road		Inverness		IV4 7HH
✱	umber)								

Names and Addresses : Table

Record: 1 of 8

Take note

Having sorted your records, you will be asked if you want to save the changes, i.e. the records sorted, when you close your table (or form).

Choose [Yes] or [No] depending on whether or not you wish to save the sort order.

When you set up an Advanced Sort (see opposite) you can either save the sorted table or you can save the criteria as a Query. This will be listed under Queries in the Database window. To save the criteria as a Query, click the Save as Query tool in the Filter, Advanced Filter/Sort dialog box, and give the query a name that reflects its purpose. Any time you open the query its criteria will be applied.

Basic steps

1 Open the **Records** menu. Choose **Filter** then **Advanced Filter/Sort**.

2 Double-click on each field required in the fields list to add it to the lower pane.

3 Select **Ascending** or **Descending Sort** order in the **Sort** row.

4 Click the **Apply/Remove Filter** tool on the Filter/Sort toolbar.

5 The sorted table is displayed.

Take note

If you need to clear existing criteria from the grid, click the Clear Grid tool ✕ then set up your sort.

Multi-level sort

If you need to sort your records on more than one field, you can perform an Advanced Sort.

Try sorting your Names and Addresses into ascending order by Town, then Surname and then First Name.

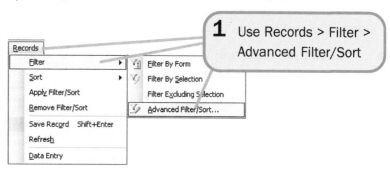

1 Use Records > Filter > Advanced Filter/Sort

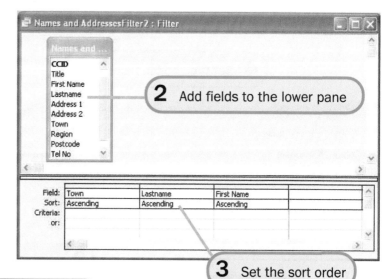

2 Add fields to the lower pane

3 Set the sort order

5 The sorted table

CCID	Title	First Name	Lastname	Address 1	Address 2	Town	Region	Postcode
3	Mr & Mrs	Brian	Jackson	Westwind Cottage	2 Whiteadder Crescent	Dalkeith	Midlothian	E22 5ZZ
1	Mrs	Ann	Jones	22 High Street		Edinburgh	Lothian	EH6 1ZZ
5	Miss	Alice	Springs	22 St John's Crescent		Edinburgh	Lothian	EH21 4WQ
7	Mr & Mr	Joe	Williamson	44 Main Road		Inverness		IV4 7HH
6	Mr	Neil	Jackson	The Auld Toll	14 Mill Wynd	Lauder	Borders	TD10 7ZZ
4	Mr & Mrs	Peter	Watson	102 Hilltop View		Lauder	Borders	TD10 ZZZ
8	Mrs	Gill	Adams	10 Blackadder Avenue		Loanhead	Midlothian	EH34 1ZZ
2	Miss	Alison	Douglas	55 West Side Way		Pencaitland	East Lothian	EH44 2PP

Record: ◄◄ ◄ 1 ► ►► ►* of 8

Find

With larger databases, it is impractical to locate records in your tables or forms by scrolling through, reading each record. The Find command will locate records that contain a specific entry in a field. Find works most efficiently if you tell it which field the data is in (so it doesn't need to search the whole table), and the field is indexed. Note these two options:

◆ **Match Case** - find only those entries that match the case used in the Find What field (capitals/lower case).

◆ **Search Fields As Formatted** - find data based on its display format rather than stored value, e.g. a monetary value stored as 3.5 but formatted £3.50.

1 Put the insertion point inside the field you want to search.

2 Click the **Find** tool [🔍].

3 Key the target data in the **Find What:** field.

4 Select the field that you want to search in from the **Look In** options.

5 Choose the **Match** option required.

6 Specify the search direction using the **Search** option.

7 Select/deselect other options as required.

8 Click [Find Next] to start the search, or to look for the next match.

9 When you have found the record click [Cancel].

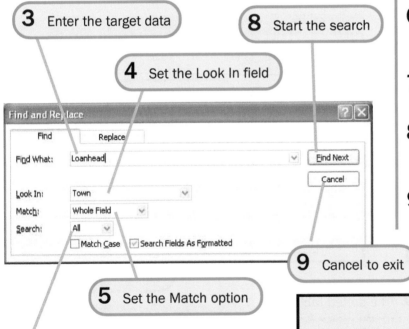

3 Enter the target data

8 Start the search

4 Set the Look In field

5 Set the Match option

6 Set the search direction

9 Cancel to exit

Take note

Database tables could have hundreds of thousands of records in them — think of the DVLC car registration database — so it is important that you can locate information quickly.

Basic steps

1 Click the **Find** tool 🔍 and go to the **Replace** tab.

2 Key the target data in **Find What:** and the replacement data in **Replace With:**

3 Specify your **Look In**, **Search** and **Match** options.

■ **Selective replace**

4 Click [Find Next].

5 Once you find the data, click [Replace].

Or

6 Click [Find Next] to move to the next occurrence.

7 Click [Cancel] when you are finished.

■ **Global replacement**

8 Click [Replace All].

9 Click [Yes] to confirm the replacement.

You can quickly change the contents of several fields using the Replace option.

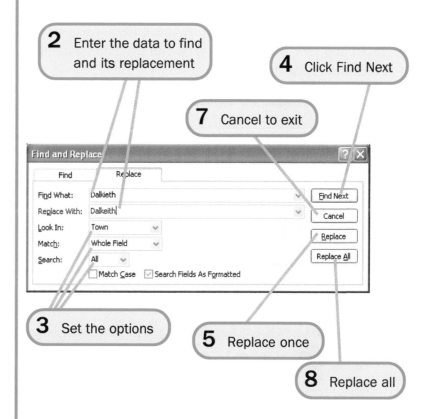

2 Enter the data to find and its replacement

4 Click Find Next

7 Cancel to exit

3 Set the options

5 Replace once

8 Replace all

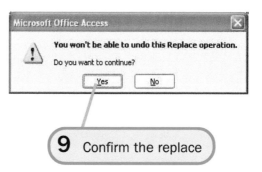

9 Confirm the replace

Filtering

Filter by Selection

When working within a table, you might want to display a subset of the records held based on some criterion, e.g. all the Books from a specific publisher. You can use Filter by Selection techniques for this.

Basic steps

1 Select the text on which you want to base your filter.

2 Click the **Filter by Selection** tool .

3 Records matching the selection are displayed.

4 Repeat the process if you want a sub-set of your new list.

5 Click the **Remove Filter** tool to display all your records again.

1 Select the text to filter on

Names and Addresses : Table

CCID	Title	First Name	Lastname	Address 1	Address 2	Town	Region
3	Mr & Mrs	Brian	Jackson	Westwind Cottage	2 Whiteadder Crescent	Dalkeith	Midlothian
1	Mrs	Ann	Jones	22 High Street		Edinburgh	Lothian
5	Miss	Alice	Springs	22 St John's Crescent		Edinburgh	Lothian
7	Mrs & Mr	Joe	Williamson	44 Main Road		Inverness	
6	Mr	Neil	Jackson	The Auld Toll	14 Mill Wynd	Lauder	Borders
4	Mr & Mrs	Peter	Watson	102 Hilltop View		Lauder	Borders
8	Mrs	Gill	Adams	10 Blackadder Avenue		Loanhead	Midlothian
2	Miss	Alison	Douglas	55 West Side Way		Pencaitland	East Lothian

Record: 2 of 8

3 The filtered subset

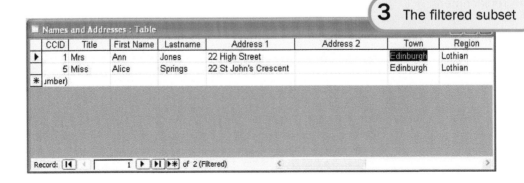

Names and Addresses : Table

CCID	Title	First Name	Lastname	Address 1	Address 2	Town	Region
1	Mrs	Ann	Jones	22 High Street		Edinburgh	Lothian
5	Miss	Alice	Springs	22 St John's Crescent		Edinburgh	Lothian

Record: 1 of 2 (Filtered)

Basic steps

1 Click the **Filter by Form** tool .

2 Select the criteria from the drop-down lists.

3 Switch to the **Or** tab and set options here if alternatives are wanted.

4 Click the **Apply Filter** tool ▽.

Filter by Form

If you wish to specify several criteria at the same time, you could use Filter by Form rather than Filter by Selection. Here you select the value to look for in a field from a drop-down list of all the values held anywhere in that field.

You can also use Filter by Form to filter by different sets of criteria simultaneously.

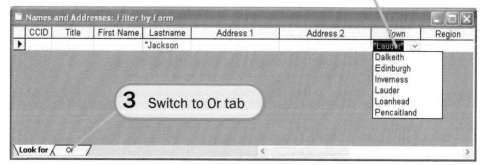

2 Select the criterion

3 Switch to Or tab

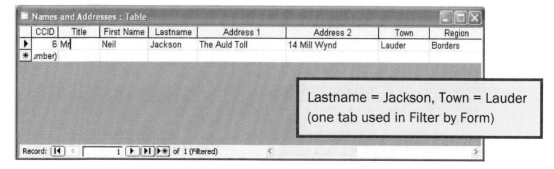

Lastname = Jackson, Town = Lauder (one tab used in Filter by Form)

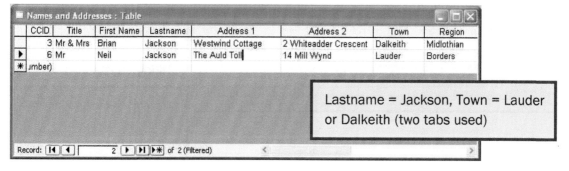

Lastname = Jackson, Town = Lauder or Dalkeith (two tabs used)

The subdatasheet

You may have noticed that in tables whose primary key is a foreign key in another table, the left-most column in the table contains a plus sign. This indicates that there is a subdatasheet of related records that can be displayed directly from that table.

You can display the related records for individual records or for all the records in the table.

Open the Book Shop database to experiment with this feature.

1 Open a table where the primary key is related to a foreign key in another table e.g. the Publisher table in the Book Shop database.

■ **Expand the subdata-sheet for a single record**

2 Click the plus sign to the left of the record.

■ **Collapse the subsheet**

3 Click the minus sign to the left of the record.

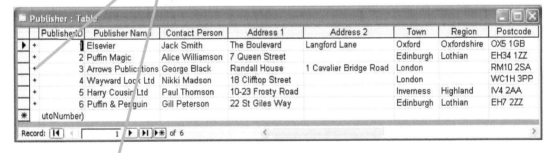

2 Click to display the subdatasheet

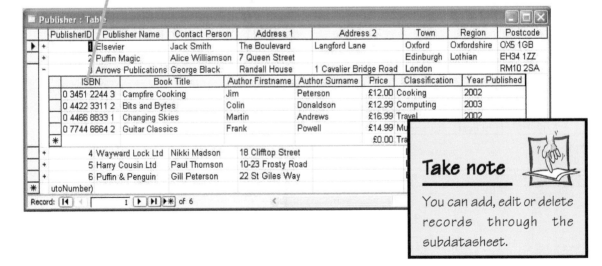

Take note

You can add, edit or delete records through the subdatasheet.

78

Expand or collapse for all records

- **Expand or collapse the subsheets for all records**

1 Open the **Format** menu.

2 Select **Subdatasheet**.

3 Choose **Expand All** or **Collapse All**.

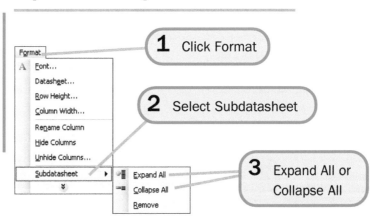

1 Click Format

2 Select Subdatasheet

3 Expand All or Collapse All

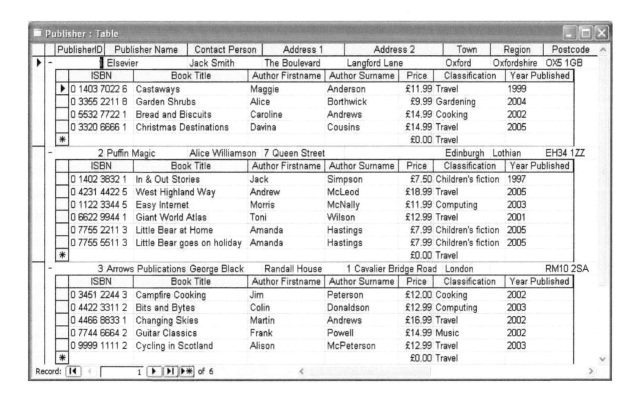

Removing and restoring a subdatasheet

You can remove the subdatasheet link if it is no longer required.

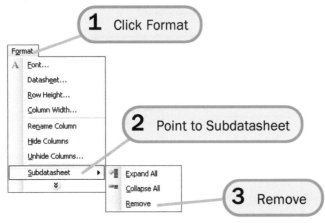

1 Click Format

2 Point to Subdatasheet

3 Remove

5 Select the table

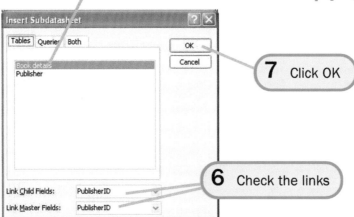

7 Click OK

6 Check the links

Basic steps

- **Remove a subsheet**
1 Open the **Format** menu.
2 Select **Subdatasheet**.
3 Choose **Remove**.
- **Restore a subsheet**
4 From the **Insert** menu choose **Subdatasheet**.
5 In the dialog box, select the table you wish to link to.
6 Check/edit the fields through which the tables are linked.
7 Click [OK].

Format a datasheet

- **Format the font**

1 Open the **Format** menu.

2 Choose **Font...**

3 Complete the dialog box.

4 Click [OK].

- **Format the datasheet**

5 Open the **Format** menu.

6 Choose **Datasheet...**

7 Complete the dialog box.

8 Click [OK].

If you wish to change the formatting on your datasheet, you can do so using the Format menu. Any changes that you make to the datasheet will be applied to the whole datasheet – you cannot change the formatting of specific rows or columns.

You can format the font used for the text, or the fill colour and gridlines of the datasheet itself.

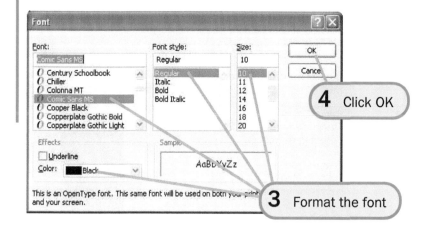

4 Click OK

3 Format the font

8 Click OK

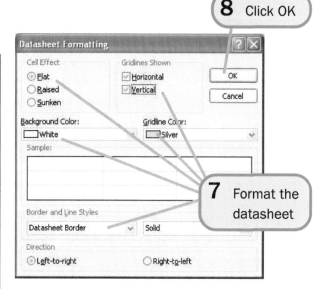

7 Format the datasheet

Take note

You can adjust the column width of individual columns by dragging the vertical bar between the field names, or by specifying the column width via the Format menu.

You can adjust the row height by dragging the horizontal bar between the records, in the row selector area, or by specifying the row height via the Format menu. All rows will be formatted to the same height.

Hide and Show

There may be times when you don't want to show all the columns in your datasheet. You may be concentrating on a task that only uses certain fields and decide to hide the ones that are of no concern at the moment.

You can always show the columns again when you need them.

■ **Hide columns**

1 Click the Field Name row to select the column.

or

2 Drag along the field name row to select a set of adjacent columns.

3 Choose **Hide Columns** from the **Format** menu.

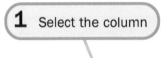
1 Select the column

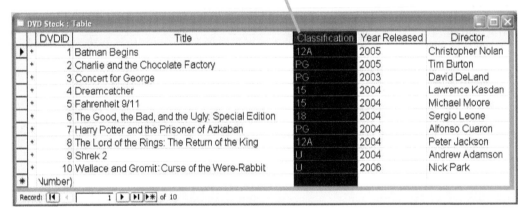

■ **Show (or hide) columns**

4 Open the **Format** menu and choose **Unhide Columns**. The **Unhide Columns** dialog box appears. The columns currently showing have a tick beside them.

5 Click on the checkbox to toggle the Show/hide status of a field.

6 Click Close when you are finished.

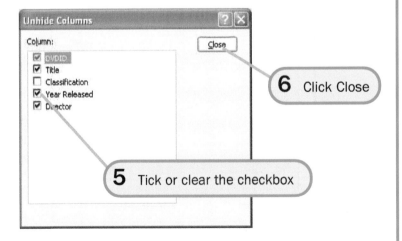
6 Click Close

5 Tick or clear the checkbox

Basic steps

- **Freeze columns**

1 Select the column(s) that you want to freeze.

2 Open the **Format** menu and choose **Freeze Columns**.

3 The columns will be moved (if necessary) and frozen at the left edge of your table.

- **Unfreeze columns**

4 Open the **Format** menu and choose **Unfreeze All Columns**.

There will be times that you need to view columns, which are distant from each other in your table, on the screen at the same time. You could do this by hiding columns that you don't need to view, or by freezing columns at the left edge of your table. Columns that have been frozen will remain at the left edge of your table while you scroll the other fields in or out of view.

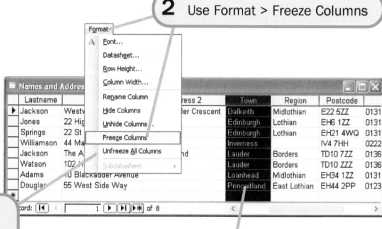

2 Use Format > Freeze Columns

1 Select the column(s)

4 Use Format > Unfreeze All Columns

3 The columns are frozen

Take note

Columns that have been frozen remain at the left edge of the table when they are unfrozen. To return one to its original position, move it – point to the field name at the top and drag and drop it – or close the table without saving the changes.

Print Preview

Now that you know how to get data into tables, and how to display specific records, you may want to print your datasheet. There are various ways to do this, but the easiest to begin with is to print from Datasheet view (this applies to either your tables, or the results from running a query).

Once the datasheet display has been formatted to your satisfaction, you can print the table.

Always do a Print Preview first, and check that the layout is okay on screen, before you commit it to paper.

Basic steps

1 Open the table you want.

2 Click the **Print Preview** tool 🔍. Your table is displayed in the Print Preview screen.

3 To edit before printing, close the Print Preview and return to Datasheet view by clicking Close on the Print Preview toolbar.

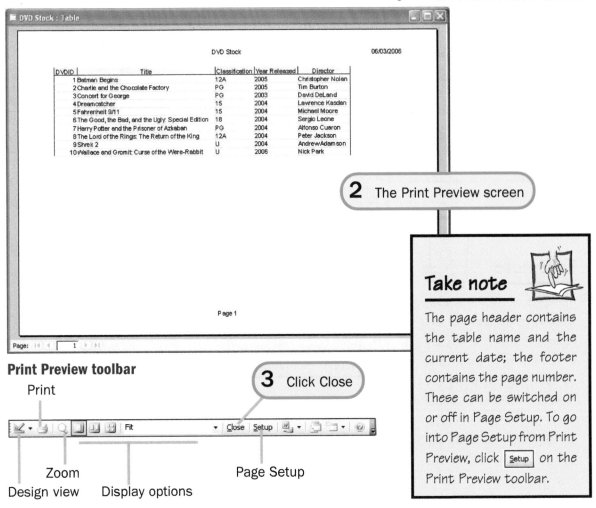

2 The Print Preview screen

3 Click Close

Print Preview toolbar

Print

Zoom

Design view   Display options

Page Setup

Take note

The page header contains the table name and the current date; the footer contains the page number. These can be switched on or off in Page Setup. To go into Page Setup from Print Preview, click Setup on the Print Preview toolbar.

Basic steps

1 Open the **File** menu.

2 Select **Page Setup**.

3 Complete the **Page Setup** dialog box as required.

4 Click [OK].

Page Setup

If you want to change the paper size, margins or orientation of your page, use the Page Setup dialog box. You can open this from Datasheet view, or from the Print Preview screen.

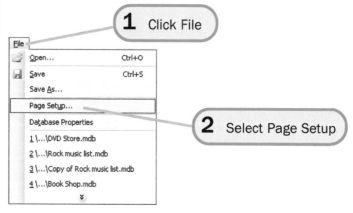

1 Click File

2 Select Page Setup

Take note

The content of the Page Setup dialog box varies from printer to printer.

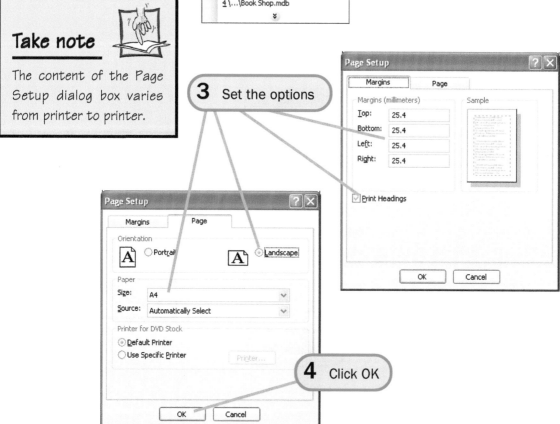

3 Set the options

4 Click OK

Print

If the table is formatted and the Page Setup is okay, you can go ahead and print your table. You can print directly from Datasheet view, or from the Print Preview screen. It does not matter which view you are in, the routine is the same.

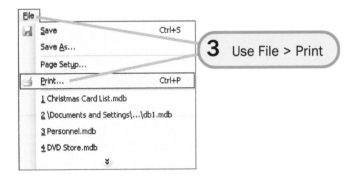

3 Use File > Print

- **Print all records**

1 Click on the Standard toolbar.

- **Print selected records**

2 Select the records.

3 Open the **File** menu and choose **Print**.

4 Complete the dialog box as required.

5 Click [OK].

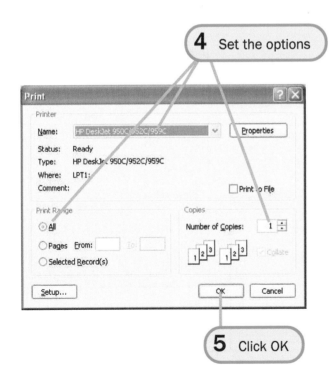

4 Set the options

5 Click OK

Take note

To select consecutive records in Datasheet view, click and drag down the selection bar to the left of the records.

Exercises

Christmas Card List database

1   Open the Christmas Card List database.

2   Open the Names and Addresses table in Datasheet view.

3   Format the font to be size 12 and blue.

4   Adjust the column width as necessary to display all data.

5   Set the row height to 17.

6   Sort the data into ascending order on Surname, then First name.

7   Freeze the Title, First name and Surname fields.

8   Hide the Telephone Number field.

9   Print out the datasheet in Landscape orientation.

10   Close the table without saving the changes.

11   Close the Christmas Card List database.

Book shop database

Task 1

1   Open the Book Shop database.

2   Open the Book details table in Datasheet view.

3   Format the datasheet to have a sunken cell effect.

4   Make the font green and bold.

5   Sort the data into descending order on Classification, then Year Published.

6   Print out the Travel books only – landscape orientation.

7   Close the table without saving the changes.

Task 1

1   Open the Publisher table in Datasheet view.

2   Freeze the Contact name and Publisher fields.

3   Use Filter by Form to select all Scottish publishers: use the criterion Region = Highland or Lothian.

4   Print out these books only, in landscape orientation.

5   Close the Publisher table without saving the changes.

6   Close the Book Shop database.

DVD store database

1   Open the DVD Store database.

2   Open the DVD Stock table in Datasheet view.

3   Use Filter by Selection to display all DVDs with a PG Classification.

4   Print the records out, in landscape orientation.

5   Remove the filter from the list.

6   Format the datasheet to have a raised effect, with a blue, bold font.

7   Hide the Director field.

8   Sort the records into ascending order on Year Released.

9   Print out the records for DVDs published in 2004 only – landscape orientation.

10 Close the DVD Store table, without saving the changes.

7 Queries

The query grid

The features discussed in Chapter 6 for filtering and sorting data are all very well if your requirements are fairly simple or you are working with one table only. However, if your requirements are more complex, queries give you a much more powerful tool to use when sorting and extracting data from your tables.

Queries are also useful if you need to extract data from more than one table.

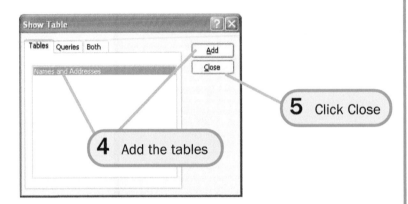

Basic steps

1 Open your Christmas Card List database.

2 Go to Queries in the Database window.

3 Double-click
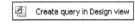.

4 Select the table(s) you want to query in the Show Table dialog box and click [Add] to add them to the query grid.

5 Click [Close].

6 The field list(s) will be displayed in the upper pane, and the query grid in the lower pane of the Query window.

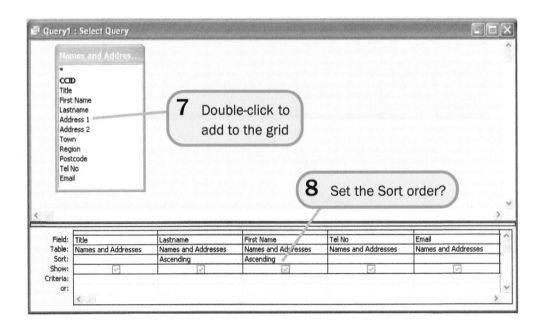

7 In the field list, double-click each field name you wish to display when you run your query – the field name will move to the query grid.

8 If you wish to sort your data, specify the Sort order for the field(s) you wish to sort in the Sort row.

9 Click to run your query.

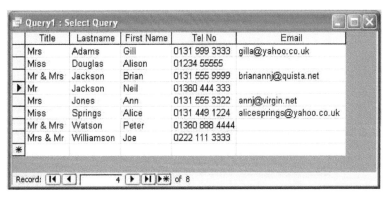

The sorted results

Take note

For more information on the Show Table dialog box see Chapter 3.

Take note

When sorting using the query grid, the sort priority works from left to right. The first level sort field e.g. Lastname must be to the left of the second level sort field, which must be to the left of the third level sort field, etc. The fields do not need to be next to each other, but they must be positioned left to right in order of priority.

Adjusting the fields in the query

You can remove fields from the grid, or move them to a different place.

- **To remove a field from the query grid**

1 Select the field (click at the top of the column).

2 Press [**Delete**].

- **To move a field**

3 Select the field.

4 Drag and drop it while pointing to the narrow bar above the field name row.

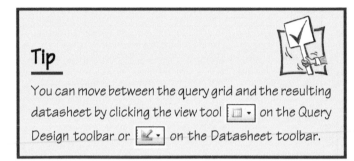

Tip

You can move between the query grid and the resulting datasheet by clicking the view tool ▢ ▾ on the Query Design toolbar or ✍ ▾ on the Datasheet toolbar.

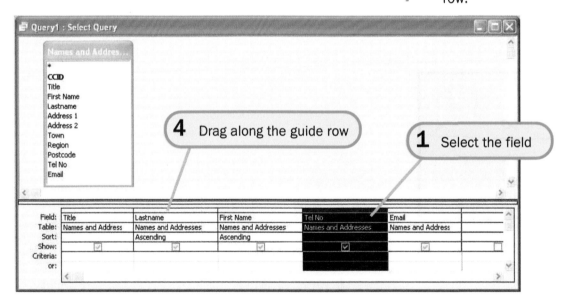

4 Drag along the guide row

1 Select the field

Field:	Title	Lastname	First Name	Tel No	Email	
Table:	Names and Address	Names and Addresses	Names and Addresses	Names and Addresses	Names and Address	
Sort:		Ascending	Ascending			
Show:	✓	✓	✓	✓	✓	
Criteria:						
or:						

Take note

Access has a powerful query tool. We will be performing queries where we specify the fields required and also the records according to the criteria set.

Saving a query

Basic steps

1 Click the **Save** tool on the Query Design or the Datasheet window

2 Give your query a name that reflects its purpose

3 Click ⬚OK⬚.

If you want to be able to re-run your query without having to set it up again, you should save it.

Saved queries will be listed in the Query area in the database window.

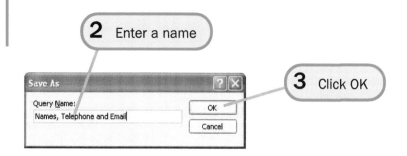

2 Enter a name

3 Click OK

Take note

To run a query again, simply double-click on it in the Database window. The results will be displayed in a datasheet.

4 Close the database

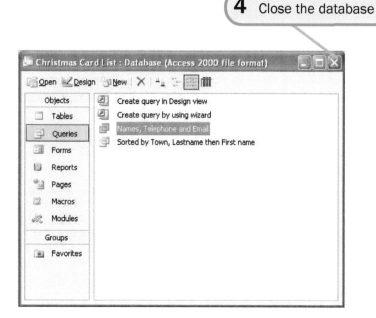

Tip

Many exam boards ask you to save your queries to provide evidence that you can complete a given task.

Multi-table queries

Multi-table queries are no more difficult than single table queries. You just have to remember to add all the tables you require to the query grid.

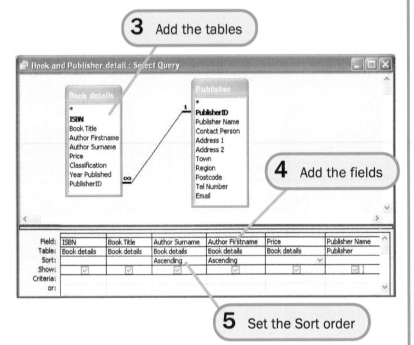

3 Add the tables

4 Add the fields

5 Set the Sort order

The output from the query

Basic steps

1 Open the Book Shop database.

2 Create a query in Design view.

3 Add the Book details table and the Publisher table to the query grid.

4 Add the fields to the query grid – ISBN, Author Surname, Author Firstname, Book Title, Price and Publisher Name.

5 Set the sort order, e.g. books into ascending order of Author Surname.

6 Save the query as Book and Publisher detail.

7 Click [!] to run it.

Basic steps

1 Create a query in Design view.

2 Add the tables required to the Design grid.

3 Select the fields.

4 Set the criteria – just type "Travel" in the criteria row for Classification. If you don't use a comparison operator (see bottom of page), Access assumes that you mean equal to.

5 Specify the sort order.

6 Save and run the query.

Take note

You don't need to type the quotes around text in the criteria row – Access will add them automatically.

Occasionally Access will add quotes to a number, or leave them off a text entry – if this happens insert or delete them using the keyboard.

Selection criteria

Criteria that you want to apply to a query can also be specified in the Query grid. They are specified in the Criteria row, below the Sort row.

We will set up a query to extract details of the Book title, Classification, Publisher and Price, of the Travel books only, with the results sorted in ascending order on Price.

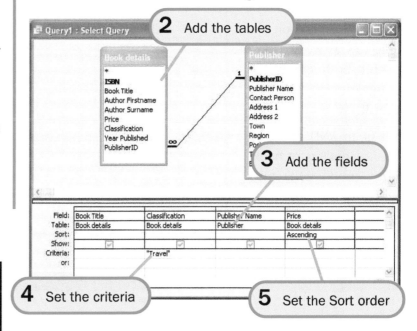

Comparison operators

When setting criteria you can use comparison operators:

>	More than	<	less than
=	Equal to	<>	not equal to
>=	More than or equal to	<=	less than or equal to

Between.... And...   Between the first and the last value (including the values)

These are mainly used for Number or Date/Time fields, but can be used with Text: > **"H"** means after H in the alphabet.

Multiple criteria

You can specify more than one criterion for your record selection. There will be times when you want records that meet multiple criteria within the same record, and other times when you want records that match one criterion or another.

All Travel books published before 2003.

Both criteria are on the same row as we are looking for both conditions being met in the one record.

This is an AND condition – we are looking for books about travel AND published before 2003.

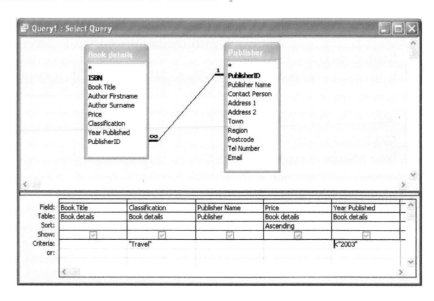

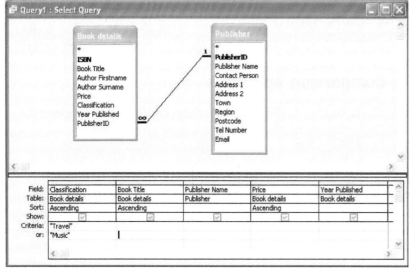

Travel books OR Music books.

This is an OR condition – we are looking for books on travel OR on music.

The example is sorted into ascending order by Classification, and then by Book Title (note the priority order on the grid).

The criteria can be entered onto separate criteria rows to show we are looking for one or the other.

Travel or Music books that cost less than £14.

Note the alternative way or entering an OR – on one criteria row.

Also, there is NO £ symbol typed into the <14.

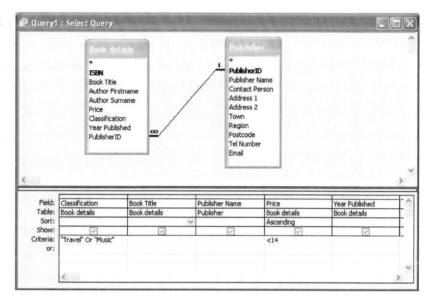

Practice

Extract details from your tables to meet the following criteria:

◆ All Cooking and Gardening books, sorted into descending order on Classification, and into ascending order on Book Title within each classification. Include the fields ISBN, Classification, Book Title, Author Surname and Price.

◆ All Travel books that cost between £10 and £14, sorted into ascending order on price. Include the fields ISBN, Classification, Book Title, Author Surname and Price.

◆ All books published by Puffin Magic, sorted into ascending order on the Book Title. Include the fields Book Title, Publisher Name and Price.

Wild card characters

There may be times when you want to perform a query based on part of a field rather than all of it. In our Book Store database, we know we have several books on the adventures of Little Bear. They have titles that follow the format *Little Bear goes Camping, Little Bear goes on Holiday*, etc. We could use a wild card in our query to extract all Little Bear books.

*   as a wild card represents a string of text

?   as a wild card represents a single character

1 Create a query in Design view.

2 Add the table to the grid – Book details.

3 Select the fields you want to display in the results – Title, Price and Year Published.

4 In the criteria row, under Title, type Little Bear*.

Access will convert this to Like "Little Bear*" when you move out of the column.

5 Save your query.

6 Run it [!].

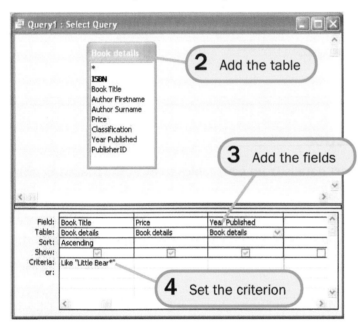

Examples of wild card use

Sm?th   Look for Smith, Smyth, etc. - any single character can replace the ?

EH4 *   Look for all postcodes that begin with EH4 e.g. EH4 1ZZ, EH4 2YY - the * can be replaced by any string of characters.

music   Look for any entry with music anywhere within in - A history of music; West End musicals; Music and dance.

*map   Look for any entry that ends with map - London Street Map; Dundee Street Map.

Basic steps

1 Create a query in Design view.

2 Add the table required to the grid – Publisher.

3 Select the fields you want to display in the results – Publisher Name, Contact Person, Tel Number and Email.

4 In the criteria row, under Email, type Is Null.

5 Save your query.

6 Run it.

■ Now display all records where you DO have email addresses for your publishers.

If you wish to extract records depending on whether they have no value or a value in a field use the Is Null or Is Not Null criteria. Is Null will return records that have an empty field, Is Not Null will return records that have an entry in the field.

Using the Publisher table we can display all publishers that have no email address.

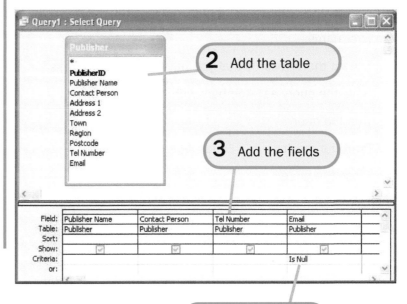

2 Add the table

3 Add the fields

4 Set the criterion

Take note

With Yes/No fields, enter Yes in the criteria row of the grid if you are looking for a selected field (a Yes), or No if you are looking for a deselected one.

Take note

There may be times when you have a field in your query grid, which you don't want to show in the result, e.g. you are looking for all records where the Town is London, but you don't want to see a whole column saying "London". You can toggle the display of a field by clicking the checkbox in the **Show** row of the grid.

Exercises

DVD Store database

Task 1

1   Open the DVD Store database.

2   Create a query in Design view, and add the Members table to the window.

3   Add the First name, Surname, Tel No and Email fields.

4   Sort the records into Ascending order by Surname, then First name.

5   Extract those records that you have an email address for.

6   Save the query as 'Members with email addresses'.

7   Run the query.

8   Print the results out in Landscape orientation.

9   Close the query.

Task 2

1   Repeat the exercise above, extracting only those records that you have NO email address for.

2   Save the query as 'Members without email addresses'.

Task 3

1   Create a query in design view, and add the DVD Stock table to the window.

2   Add all fields to the query grid.

3   Extract all records with a PG Classification, released after 2003.

4   Save the query as 'PG films since 2003'.

5   Run the query then close it.

Task 4

1   Create a query in Design view, and add the Loans table to the window.

2 Add all fields to the query grid.

3 Extract details of members who have NOT paid for their loan.

4 Save the query as 'Payment outstanding'.

5 Run the query then close it.

Task 5

1 Create a query in Design view and add the Members, DVD Stock and Loan tables to the window.

2 Add the Loan ID, Members name, Telephone No, Email address, DVD Title and Paid fields to the grid.

3 Sort the records by Surname then First name.

4 Extract details of all members who have paid for their loans.

5 Save the query as 'Payment received'.

6 Run the query then close it.

Task 6

1 Extract details of all members living in an EH2 postcode area, with no email address.

2 Display the member name, postcode and email address in the result.

3 Save the query as 'EH2'.

4 Run and close the query.

Task 7

1 Create a query to display all non-child members.

2 Display the Surname, First name, Title, Return date and Paid fields in the result.

3 Sort the results in ascending order on Title then Return date.

4 Save the query as 'Adult members'.

5 Run the query then close it.

Task 8

1 Create a query to display all details from the DVD Stock table, for DVDs released between 2002 and 2004, sorted in ascending order on Title.

2 Save the query as 'Released between 2002 and 2004'.

3 Run the query then close it.

4 Close the DVD Store database.

Personnel database

Task 1

1 Open the Personnel database.

2 Create a query to display the names, job titles and salaries of all staff earning over £22,000.

3 Sort the results in descending salary order.

4 Save the query as 'Salary over £22,000'.

5 Run the query then close it.

Task 2

1 Create a query to display the name, department and course start date of all staff on the BITS course.

2 In the result, display the course name in full, rather then the BITS code.

3 Save the query as 'BITS course trainees'.

4 Run the query then close it.

Task 3

1 Create a query to extract details of all members of staff whose surname begins with 'S'.

2 Display the staff name (in full), job title, department and salary in the result.

3 Sort the results in ascending order on Salary.

4 Save the query as 'Surname S'.

5 Run the query then close it.

6 Close the Personnel database.

102

8 Reports

Creating reports

Reports allow you to specify how you want the data in your tables and queries printed. Many of the techniques used are similar or the same as those found in Form design. There are, however, a number of summary features that are unique to reports, and they are what we will look at in this chapter.

Reports can be created in a number of ways – using AutoReport, a Report wizard, or directly in the Design view of the report.

Any reports that you save will be listed under Reports in the Database window.

AutoReport

A simple report can be created quickly using the AutoReport feature. Try creating an AutoReport for the table in your Christmas Card List database

Basic steps

1 Open your database.

2 Display the tables in the Database window.

3 Select the table – Names and Addresses – to create a report for.

4 Click the **AutoReport** tool in the New Object list.

A simple report will be displayed, showing the records in a column down the page.

5 To print your report, click the **Print** tool on the Print Preview toolbar.

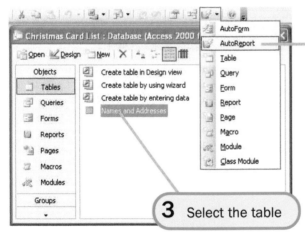

3 Select the table

4 Click AutoReport

Take note

You can move from page to page in your report using the navigation buttons at the bottom of the preview window.

Save and close a report

1 Open the **File** menu and choose **Save**.

2 Give the report a meaningful name.

3 Click [OK].

4 Close the Preview window and return to the Database window – click [x] in the top right or [Close] on the Print Preview toolbar.

■ **From Print Design view**

5 Click the **Save** tool [🖫] on the Report Design toolbar.

6 Repeat steps 2–3 above.

7 Close the Report Design window.

You will find your report listed in the Report area in the Database window.

If you wish to keep your report so that you can reuse it you must save it.

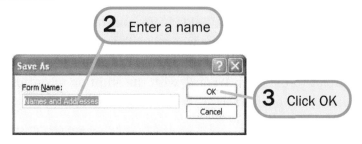

2 Enter a name

3 Click OK

Take note

Many of the features discussed in relation to the Form Design window (Chapter 5) also apply to the Report Design window, e.g.

◆ Formatting field controls

◆ Toggling the display of the field list and toolbox

◆ Adding a report header/footer (appears at top of page 1 and end of last page) – see the View menu in Report Design

◆ Adding a page header/footer (repeated at top and bottom of each page)

◆ Adding labels and pictures.

Tip

You can move between Print Preview and Report Design view by clicking the View tool on the Print Preview [☑•] or Report Design [▣•] toolbar.

Report Wizard

As an alternative to using AutoReport to create a report, you could create a report using the Report Wizard feature.

You can select specific fields from your tables and/or queries as you work through the wizard (rather than having all fields as is the case with the AutoReport). The Report Wizard is very similar to the Form Wizard, with the addition of options that allow you to summarise the data in your report.

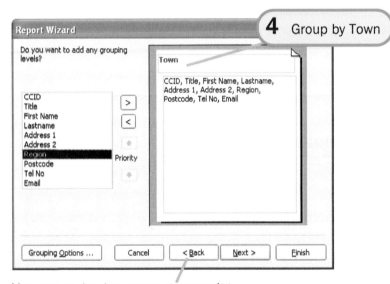

You can go back a stage at any point

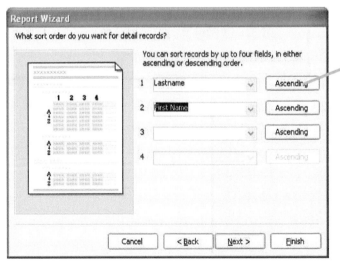

1 Go to the **Reports** area in the Database window and double-click

> Create report by using wizard .

2 From the list select the Table that you want to create a report for – Names and addresses.

The fields in the table will be displayed in the **Available fields** list.

3 Add all fields to the **Selected Fields** list and click Next > .

4 Group the records by Town. Click Next > .

4 Group by Town

5 Define the Sort

5 Sort the records by Lastname and then First name then click Next >.

6 Set the **Page Orientation** to Landscape, and choose a layout.

7 Select the **Adjust the field width...** checkbox and click Next >.

8 Choose a style and click Next >.

9 Edit the name if needed.

10 Select **Preview** the report and click Finish.

11 Print the report if you wish.

12 Close the Christmas Card List database.

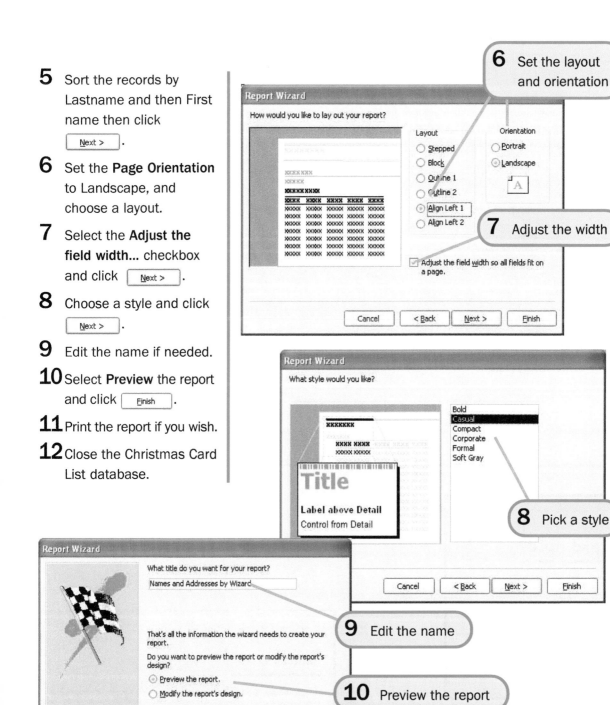

6 Set the layout and orientation

7 Adjust the width

8 Pick a style

9 Edit the name

10 Preview the report

Names and Addresses by Wizard

Town	Dalkeith								
Lastname	**First Name**	**CCID**	**Title**	**Address 1**	**Address 2**	**Region**	**Postc**	**Tel No**	**Email**
Jackson	Brian	3	Mr & Mr	Westwind Cottag	2 Whiteadder Cre	Midlothian	E22 5	0131 55	briananni@quista.net

Town	Edinburgh								
Lastname	**First Name**	**CCID**	**Title**	**Address 1**	**Address 2**	**Region**	**Postc**	**Tel No**	**Email**
Jones	Ann	1	Mrs	22 High Street		Lothian	EH6 1	0131 55	annj@virgin.net
Springs	Alice	5	Miss	22 St John's Cres		Lothian	EH21	0131 44	alicesprings@yahoo.co

Town	Inverness								
Lastname	**First Name**	**CCID**	**Title**	**Address 1**	**Address 2**	**Region**	**Postc**	**Tel No**	**Email**
Williamson	Joe	7	Mrs & M	44 Main Road			IV4 7H	0222 11	

Town	Lauder								
Lastname	**First Name**	**CCID**	**Title**	**Address 1**	**Address 2**	**Region**	**Postc**	**Tel No**	**Email**
Jackson	Neil	6	Mr	The Auld Toll	14 Mill Wynd	Borders	TD10	01360 4	
Watson	Peter	4	Mr & Mr	102 Hilltop View		Borders	TD10	01360 8	

Town	Loanhead								
Lastname	**First Name**	**CCID**	**Title**	**Address 1**	**Address 2**	**Region**	**Postc**	**Tel No**	**Email**
Adams	Gill	8	Mrs	10 Blackadder Av		Midlothian	EH34	0131 99	gilla@yahoo.co.uk

10 March 2006

Take note

If you select your fields from more than one table, an additional option "How do you want to view your data" is given before the Grouping option.

Take note

If you wish to print specific pages from a report, open the File menu and choose Print, then specify the pages required in the dialog box.

Basic steps

1 Create a report using the Report Wizard.

2 Use the Book and Publisher detail query.

3 Add all fields to the report, and view the data by Publisher.

4 Do not group the data.

5 Sort the records into Ascending order by Book Title.

6 Click the **Summary Options ...** button.

7 Select the **Sum** checkbox for the Price field.

8 Show the **Detail and Summary** if you want the price summed for each Publisher, and also for the total report.

Or

9 Show the **Summary Only** if you want the price summed for the whole report, but not each publisher.

10 Click [OK].

11 Complete the wizard.

12 View your report in Print Preview.

Summary calculations

As well as grouping your data into logical sets in a report e.g. by Publisher, or Town, you can also perform summary calculations on the data within each set. For example we could produce a report that listed all the books from each publisher and calculate the total value of the books, or the minimum, maximum or average price of the books.

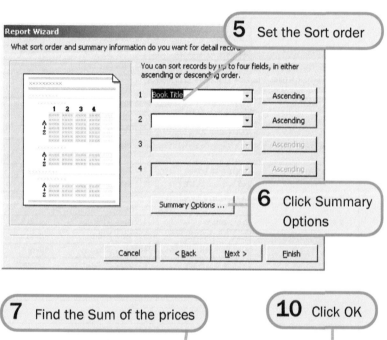

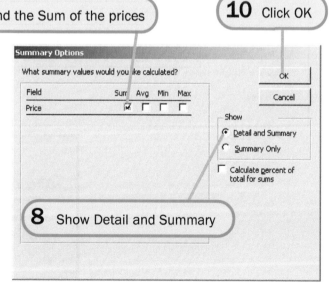

Report listing all the books from each publisher, with the total
values of the books for each, and overall.

Publisher with Price summed

Publisher Name	Book Title	ISBN	Author Surna	Author Firstna	Price
Arrows Publications	Bits and Bytes	0 4422 3311	Donaldson	Colin	£12.99
	Campfire Cooking	0 3451 2244	Peterson	Jim	£12.00
	Changing Skies	0 4466 8833	Andrews	Martin	£16.99
	Cycling in Scotland	0 9999 1111	McPeterson	Alison	£12.99
	Guitar Classics	0 7744 6664	Powell	Frank	£14.99

Summary for 'Publisher Name' = Arrows Publications (5 detail records)
Sum   £69.96

Elsevier	Bread and Biscuits	0 5532 7722	Andrews	Caroline	£14.99
	Castaways	0 1403 7022	Anderson	Maggie	£11.99
	Christmas Destinations	0 3320 6666	Cousins	Davina	£14.99
	Garden Shrubs	0 3355 2211	Borthwick	Alice	£9.99

Summary for 'Publisher Name' = Elsevier (4 detail records)
Sum   £51.96

Harry Cousin Ltd	Crazy Comets	0 4433 2233	Custard	William	£20.00
	Jazz and Blues Highlights	0 7733 2200	French	Gordon	£12.75
	The Western Isles	0 9922 3322	Littlejohn	Tracy	£14.99

Summary for 'Publisher Name' = Harry Cousin Ltd (3 detail records)
Sum   £47.74

Puffin & Penguin	Penguins on Parade	1 2222 2222	Lawrence	Amanda	£8.99
	Puffins go on Holiday	1 3333 3333	Simpson	Jane	£7.95

Summary for 'Publisher Name' = Puffin & Penguin (2 detail records)
Sum   £16.94

Puffin Magic	Easy Internet	0 1122 3344	McNally	Morris	£11.99
	Giant World Atlas	0 6622 9944	Wilson	Toni	£12.99
	In & Out Stories	0 1402 3832	Simpson	Jack	£7.50
	Little Bear at Home	0 7755 2211	Hastings	Amanda	£7.99
	Little Bear goes on holiday	0 7755 5511	Hastings	Amanda	£7.99
	West Highland Way	0 4231 4422	McLeod	Andrew	£18.99

Summary for 'Publisher Name' = Puffin Magic (6 detail records)
Sum   £67.45

Wayward Lock Ltd	Ballet music from Russia	0 5555 2233	Black	Stephen	£15.99
	Cycling in Holland	0 4422 1212	Wilson	Toni	£14.75
	Outdoor Adventures	0 9933 2255	Donaldson	Francis	£9.75

Summary for 'Publisher Name' = Wayward Lock Ltd (3 detail records)
Sum   £40.49

Grand Total   **£294.54**

Take note

The Price field has been summed for each Publisher,
and the total value of all books has been calculated
and displayed at the end of the report.

Exercises

Book Shop database

1   Open the Book Shop database.

2   Create a report using the Report Wizard, based on the Book and Publisher detail query. All fields should be displayed on the report.

3   Select By Publisher at the How do you want to view the data options.

4   Do not add a grouping option.

5   Sort the records into ascending order on Price.

6   Select the orientation, layout and style options required – experiment with them.

7   Preview your report.

8   Go into Design view for your report.

9   Add a suitable image to the report header area.

10   Set the Size Mode option to zoom.

11   Save your report and preview it.

12   Close the Book Shop database.

DVD store database

1   Open the DVD Store database.

2   Create a report using the Report Wizard.

3   Add these fields to the Selected Fields list.

MemberID, First name and *Surname* from the *Members* table

Title from the *DVD Stock* table

Rental Price, Return Date and *Paid* from the Loan table

4   View the data by DVD Stock.

5   Group the data by Return date – check the grouping options and group by Month.

6   Sort the report into ascending order by Surname.

7   In the Summary Options… sum the price field to show the income that should have been generated each month, and also the total income.

8   Set the page orientation to Landscape.

9   Specify the other options as required.

10 Preview your report. The potential rental income for each DVD for each Month should be displayed, and the total income should be displayed at the end of the report.

11 Close the DVD Store database.

Personnel database

1   Open the Personnel database.

2   Create a report using the Report Wizard.

3   Add these fields to the Selected Fields list:

    StaffID, *Firstname* and *Surname* from the Staff table

    Course Title from the Courses table

    Course Start Date from the Course Bookings table

4   View the data by Courses.

5   Do not specify a grouping level.

6   Sort the results into ascending order by Surname, then Firstname.

7   Specify the other options as you wish.

8   Preview your report.

9   Add an image to the report header. Set the size mode option to zoom.

10 Save the changes and preview your report.

11 Close the Personnel database.

Index

Printed and bound by CPI Group (UK) Ltd, Croydon, CR0 4YY

22/10/2024

01777635-0010